HERSHEY'S
1934 Cookbook

Revised and expanded with chocolate recipes
brought up to date for use in today's kitchen

Published by
Hershey Chocolate Company
A Division of
 **Hershey Foods Corporation**

Twelfth Printing

■ *Thirty-seven years ago, in 1934, Hershey published
its own chocolate cookbook, filled with all kinds of
wonderful chocolate desserts. It is from this source that
many of the recipes have been taken and brought up to
date for you to use today. We've revised some of the
recipes, and added some others. Margarine wasn't
widely used when the first Hershey book was published.
Many other things that make baking easier for you
than your mother, including electric blenders and
no-stick pans, were not even around. Even though
the method of baking has become more convenient,
the end product remains essentially the same.
Hershey's test kitchens have taken painstaking care
to assure the same wonderful flavor that has
become a trademark of Hershey baked products
throughout the years. We hope you enjoy the
recipes, we hope you enjoy the book.*

Photos on pages 6-15: The Bettmann Archive, Brown Brothers, Culver Pictures, Underwood and Underwood.

CHOCOLATE HINTS

- Hershey's Cocoa may be used in place of baking chocolate. 3 Tablespoons of Hershey's Cocoa plus 1 Tablespoon of shortening or oil equals 1 ounce (1 square) of baking chocolate.

- Do not substitute Hershey's Baking Chips or Milk Chocolate for Hershey's Baking Chocolate in recipes.

- Chocolate easily absorbs odors from other foods. Therefore, wrap tightly and store in a cool, dry place (not over 78° F.).

- Bloom, the gray film that appears on chocolate, occurs when chocolate is exposed to varying temperatures. It does not affect the taste or quality of the chocolate.

- Chocolate scorches easily, therefore, melt Hershey's Baking Chocolate or Baking Chips in the top of a double boiler over simmering water or in a small saucepan set in a pan of hot water.

- Melt Hershey's Milk Chocolate in the top of a double boiler over hot, not boiling, water. High temperatures cause milk chocolate to stiffen.

- Beat hot chocolate beverages with a rotary beater until foamy to prevent formation of a skin and to enhance flavor.

- Prevent skin from forming on the top of cooked puddings and pie fillings by pressing waxed paper onto surface before cooling.

- Accurately measure Hershey's Cocoa by *lightly* packing cocoa into measuring cup and leveling with a spatula.

- For even consistency, shake Hershey's Chocolate Flavored Syrup before opening the can.

- It is desirable to store an open can of Hershey's Chocolate Flavored Syrup in the refrigerator. Should it become thicker than desired, place can in lukewarm water and stir.

- Chocolate deflates stiffly beaten egg white mixtures, so fold in carefully—just until blended.

- For chocolate curls, draw blade of vegetable parer over smooth side of a slightly warm block of Hershey's Baking Chocolate or Special Dark Chocolate Bar.

- In recipes, Hershey's Baking Chocolate, cut into pieces, should be broken into pieces about the size of almonds.

- When melting chocolate for coating and dipping candy centers, be sure all utensils are completely dry. Also, when adding a shortening to the chocolate to make it more liquid, use only vegetable shortening, not butter or margarine.

Contents

Chocolate Marshmallow
Pudding 58
Chocolate Syrup Mousse 59
Chocolate Trifle 55
Cocoa Cream Tapioca 51
Cocoa Meringue Cake 58
Mocha Chocolate Marlow 59
Old-Fashioned Chocolate
Ice Cream 50
Steamed Chocolate Pudding 56

Breads
Chocolate Chip Orange
Muffins 62
Chocolate Dessert Waffles 65
Chocolate Tea Bread 65
Orange-Cocoa Afternoon Tea
Biscuits 62
Raisin-Nut Cocoa Bread 63
Spiced Cocoa Doughnuts 63

Cookies
Blue Ribbon Fruit Cookies 74
Carol's Chocolate Cocoanut
Squares 68
Chocolate Almond Nuggets 72
Chocolate Cocoanut
Macaroons 74
Chocolate Date and Nut Bars 72
Chocolate Fruit Cookies 75
Chocolate Midgets 69
Chocolate Pinks 70
Chocolate Robins 69
Chocolate Syrup Brownies 70
Chocolate Walnut Wheels 73
Cocoa Bread Crumb Cookies 74
Cocoa Candy Cakes 75
Cocoa-Molasses Drop Cakes 69
Hershey's Chocolatetown
Chip Cookies 75
Mini Chip Sugar Cookies 68

Candies
Angel Fudge 82
Chocolate Cherry Cordials 85
Chocolate Chip-Peanut Butter
Fudge 83
Chocolate Cocoanut Balls 86
Chocolate Cocoanut Squares 80
Chocolate Log Cabin Rolls 79
Chocolate Nut Clusters 80
Chocolate Peanut Butter
Fudge 86
Chocolate Pecan Pralines 79
Chocolate Popcorn Balls 84
Chocolate Potato Candy 87
Chocolate Seafoam 83
Chocolate Turkish Paste 84
Country Club Two-Story
Fudge 78
Creamy Cocoa Taffy 87
Fudge Caramels 80

Beverages
Chocolate Egg Nog 95
Chocolate Malted Milk 94
Chocolate Pineapple Freeze 90
Chocolate Syrup Iced
Chocolate 91
Cocomoko Float 90
Five O'Clock Whipped
Chocolate 94
Frosted Chocolate Shake 90
Hot Cocoa 92
Hot Cocoa for a Crowd 92
Mint Cocoa Cup 95
Mulled Cocoa Cup 92
Orange Chocolate Float 90
Rich Iced Chocolate 91
Royal Hot Chocolate 94
Spanish Chocolate 95

Remember When–
The Early 1930's

The 1930's. A decade of mixed blessings. Herbert Hoover was about to vacate the White House to be replaced by President-elect Roosevelt. The population of the United States was approximately 123 million people, and 53 million of them still lived on farms. Unemployment was creeping upwards to 25% of the labor force and, for those who worked, the hourly wage was 44¢. Economically we were in one of the worst periods of our lives, politically we were in a turmoil, and socially we looked about for any panacea that would temporarily remove our fears.

Life in the United States in the early 1930's was in a
state of chaos, but the optimistic American remained dedicated
to the hope that "things would get better." In the interim,
it was necessary to "make do" while waiting for prosperity
to come from "just around the corner." For one-third of the
nation, necessities meant food, shelter and a job; for the
remaining two-thirds it meant a home, meat on the table,
a car, a radio and a regular Saturday night trip to the movies.
After the movies, it might have meant a jaunt to a local
tavern. Although prohibition had been in effect for 13 years,
the absolute curtailment of an established social custom was
just too unwieldy to enforce. In the early 1930's, prohibition
was to have run its course, and the 18th Amendment was
about to be repealed, ushered along with the tune of "Happy
Days Are Here Again." For the Government, repeal of the
18th Amendment was a necessity needed to generate revenue
for the Federal coffers. For the average American, repeal
served as an indicator that things were possibly getting better
in the home.

The home in the early 1930's ranged anywhere from a two room walk-up, with running water and sporadic coal heating, to a rambling 5-bedroom Victorian, that was passed down through the family. For the most part, however, the average home consisted of 6 rooms, a bath, a one-car detached garage, at a cost of around $2,500. Even though the garage came with the house, it may or may not have contained an automobile. If it did, it was anything from a 1925 Chevrolet that was five years old and had cost $825 new, to a 1930 Ford coupe that cost $600. America in 1930 was tightening her purse strings, and a new car every other year was considered luxury for only the very rich. The garages in many homes, in fact, garaged no car at all and masqueraded as a food cellar for home-jarred fruits and vegetables. Preparing and preserving peaches, cherries, pears and string beans was done not only for the pleasure it gave the homemaker, but because "store-bought" fruits and vegetables were becoming much too expensive. If the garage was not used as a pantry for home-prepared foods, it was, in dire extremes, used as an extra bedroom and a place to sleep for "Uncle Louis who was laid off his job in the automobile factory in Detroit." An ironic fate in an ironic era.

The living room of the American home at the beginning
of the decade with its large easy chairs, high-back sofas
with doilies on the arm rest and antimacassars on the back,
slightly worn rugs and colored prints on the wall were all
accoutrements to the mainstay of American family life, the
radio. Radios in the 30's ranged from a small console ($19.95)
to an "Oxford Hepplewhite de luxe highboy with sliding
doors, American walnut finish with Australian lacewood
paneling" ($150, not counting tubes; Western prices slightly
higher). Through the brown box in the living room came the
voices of "Amos 'n' Andy" in their nightly 15-minute sketch
(Monday–Friday 7:00 EST NBC Red Network), the melodic
chirps of the "Songbird of the South," Kate Smith ("Hello
Everybody") and the voice of the adventurous Lowell Thomas.
The radio, indeed, commanded an incredible audience. It

was everyone's passkey to adventure, music, laughter and news at least five nights a week.

On a Saturday night it was typical for most Americans to take leave from their radios in the living room and further escape into the celluloid realm of Hollywood. In the 1930's an estimated 60-million people weekly walked, rode and ran to the neighborhood Bijou, Orpheum or Rex, paid their admission (adults 25¢, children 10¢) and watched with total involvement the plights and romances of their cinematic idols. In the 30's you could hear your idols talk, sing, yell and cry, with an appropriate background of canned music. Gone were the titled screens, and gone were the theater orchestras, a situation loudly declaimed by the American Federation of Musicians ("I went to the Canned Goods Fair, the prunes and the tunes were there . . ."). Though of poor quality, sound was in, and so were the idols it created. Clark Gable, Will Rogers, Janet Gaynor, Joan Crawford, Norma Shearer, Wallace Beery, Mae West, W. C. Fields were all familiar names to moviegoers. When they died a tragic death or lost a forlorn lover, the audience in the pathos of the moment was totally empathetic, an empathy that somehow overshadowed the troubles of their own lives. Besides the

escapism that the movies offered, they sometimes offered
more tangible rewards. The era of the "talkies" was the era
of the promotion. Giveaways at local theaters ("Dish night:
Collect a complete set of fine dinnerware completely free")
hastened the return of moviegoers week after week. No
matter that it took at least a year to collect a complete set,
it was free and anything that was free in the 1930's received
a warm welcome. Almost as warm a welcome as the Sunday
papers and the comic adventures of the rotogravured heroes
who inhabited them.

The most popular reading matter of the day was by far

the Sunday comics. In spite of the success of the *Literary Digest, Vanity Fair,* the *Saturday Evening Post, The American Mercury* and *Liberty Magazine* ("reading time 12 minutes 35 seconds"), they were all overshadowed in the average home by Little Orphan Annie ("Arf" says Sandy) and her Sunday sidekicks. Dick Tracy, Gasoline Alley, Maggie & Jiggs and a host of others warmed the hearts of Americans in the 1930's, first in the comics and later in radio, novels and Big-Little Books. America's heroes may have been on paper, but to the reading audience they were real, a curiosity which sometimes diminished the problems of the times and most of all the problems of the American housewife.

The American housewife in the 1930's, with the economy the way it was, had an extremely difficult job. She was expected to make do for her family in times when there was little or no money coming in. Economy and thrift were the watch words of the day. All the everyday purchases, whether for dinner, cleaning, dressing or general housework, were made with an eye on the pocketbook. Meals were planned around the general staples sold by the local butcher and baker, and with vegetables and fruits that were canned

at home. (In the 1930's sirloin steak sold for 29¢ a pound, bacon was 11¢ a pound, potatoes were 2¢ a pound and bread was 5¢ a loaf.) Soup, selling at 12¢ a can and serving four, augmented many a meal. Soup with her own vegetables added, in many instances, was the meal. For the most part, keeping the house clean was a manual job done with polish, yellow soap and a lot of elbow grease. Keeping the insects away was done with Flit ("quick, Henry, the Flit"). Carpet sweepers cleaned the rugs in as much as vacuum cleaners complete with attachments were still a little bit too expensive. (A 1932 Hoover, with attachments, sold for $79.50.) The wash was generally done in an electric washing machine ($47.95) and, although a welcome replacement for the scrubboard, it took its toll in many a finger caught in the wringer. The homemaker, with all her other chores, was also a "cottage industry" in terms of clothing for the family. Although the sewing machine (the Singer with the treadle) was an expensive purchase, it more than paid for itself in terms of clothes, clothes that were worn and then passed down to a younger brother or sister.

The kitchen of the American home of the 1930's was the domain of the housewife. Besides being a place for preparation and preserving, it was also the place where countless hours were spent baking. Cookies, cakes, pies, icings and frostings were made—and "from scratch" (an event of much pleasure to younger members of the family who got to lick the mixing bowl). Mixing was done with either an electric mixer ($9.95), or more popularly with an egg beater, a bowl and spoon. All the natural ingredients were used (butter was 28¢ a pound, milk 10¢ a quart, eggs were 29¢ a dozen and sugar was 5¢ a pound). When she baked with chocolate, more often than not, she used Hershey's chocolate products. In the 1930's the Hershey Chocolate Company was making products for baking, as it had been for some 30 years. Cocoa, Baking Chocolate, Chocolate Syrup and Milk Chocolate Bars were all to be found in the kitchen of almost every American home. Recipes were original, passed down for generations, or gleaned from a Hershey Chocolate Cookbook. No matter what the source, the finished products were the best ever made, and nobody could bake like your mother. Except for you, when you turn these pages.

Cakes

Demon Cake (page 18)

DEMON CAKE

4 squares Hershey's Baking Chocolate . . . 1 cupful butter . . .
2¼ cupfuls granulated sugar . . . 1½ cupfuls buttermilk or
sour milk . . . 3 cupfuls sifted cake flour . . . 1 teaspoonful
baking soda . . . ½ teaspoonful baking powder . . .
½ teaspoonful salt . . . 5 eggs, separated . . . 1 teaspoonful
vanilla.

Melt the baking chocolate over simmering water, and
add to the butter and sugar creamed together well. Add
buttermilk and flour which has been sifted with the
baking soda, baking powder and salt alternately, then
add the well-beaten egg yolks and the egg whites, stiffly
whipped, and lastly the vanilla. Pour into 3 well-greased
and floured 9-inch cake pans. Bake in moderate oven
(350 degrees) for 30 to 35 minutes. Put together with
Fluffy Vanilla Icing (page 35).

CREOLE CHOCOLATE CAKE

3 squares Hershey's Baking Chocolate . . . ½ cupful granulated
sugar . . . 1 cupful milk . . . 1 egg . . . ½ cupful butter . . .
1 cupful granulated sugar . . . 3 eggs . . . 1 teaspoonful
vanilla . . . 2 cupfuls flour (all-purpose) . . . 1 tablespoonful
baking powder . . . dash of cinnamon.

Melt the baking chocolate, and add ½ cupful sugar and
the milk. Cook in top of double boiler till well blended;
remove from the fire and add 1 well-beaten egg. Stir
well and cool slightly. Cream butter and 1 cupful sugar;
add 3 eggs, beaten well, and then the chocolate mixture
and vanilla. Add the flour sifted with the baking powder
and cinnamon. Beat well. Pour into 2 greased and floured
9-inch layer pans, and bake in a moderate oven (350
degrees) 25 to 30 minutes. Frost cake with Creole Icing
(page 31).

HERSHEY'S SPECIAL CAKE

½ cupful butter . . . 1½ cupfuls granulated sugar, sifted . . .
2 eggs, unbeaten . . . 2 cupfuls sifted cake flour . . .
½ teaspoonful salt . . . 1 cupful sour milk . . . 3 squares
Hershey's Baking Chocolate, melted . . . 1 teaspoonful baking
soda . . . 1 tablespoonful vinegar.

Cream butter, add sugar gradually and cream them
together. Add 1 egg and beat well. Add second egg and
beat well. Sift flour and salt, and add alternately with
milk, beating well. Add melted baking chocolate. Add
baking soda which has been dissolved in the vinegar.
Beat well. Pour into 2 well-buttered 9-inch layer pans.
Bake in moderate oven (375 degrees) 25 minutes. Cool.
Cover with Aunt Jessie's Chocolate Icing (page 30).

OLD-FASHIONED COCOA MINT CAKE

⅔ cupful butter . . . 1⅔ cupfuls granulated sugar . . . 3 eggs
. . . 2 cupfuls flour (all-purpose) . . . ⅔ cupful Hershey's Cocoa
. . . 1¼ teaspoonfuls baking soda . . . ¼ teaspoonful baking
powder . . . 1 teaspoonful salt . . . 1⅓ cupfuls milk . . .
½ cupful crushed peppermint candy.

Cream butter, sugar and eggs until fluffy, and beat
vigorously 3 minutes (high speed of mixer). Combine
flour, cocoa, baking soda, baking powder and salt; add
alternately with milk to creamed mixture. Blend in
crushed candy. Pour batter into 2 greased and floured
9-inch cake pans. Bake in a moderate oven (350 degrees)
for 35 minutes. Cool 10 minutes before removing from
pans. Ice cake with Cocoa Peppermint Icing (page 32).

UPSIDE-DOWN CHOCOLATE CAKE

2 tablespoonfuls butter . . . ½ cupful brown sugar, packed
. . . 1 can (1 pound) apricot halves, drained . . . 8 to 10
maraschino cherries, halved . . . ⅓ cupful butter . . .
¾ cupful granulated sugar . . . ¼ cupful Hershey's Cocoa . . .
dash of cinnamon . . . 2 eggs . . . 1¾ cupfuls sifted cake
flour . . . 1 teaspoonful baking soda . . . ¾ cupful milk . . .
½ teaspoonful vanilla.

Melt 2 tablespoonfuls butter in a heavy frying pan or
9-inch square pan. Add brown sugar, then arrange the
apricot halves all over the bottom of pan on the brown
sugar, placing cherry halves between. Set aside while
preparing the cake. For cake: cream the ⅓ cupful butter,
granulated sugar, cocoa and cinnamon; add eggs, beaten
very little, and whip the mixture vigorously. Then add
flour and baking soda, sifted together, alternately with
the milk. Add vanilla and pour batter into the pan over
the fruit. Bake in a moderate oven (350 degrees) 35 to
40 minutes. Turn out immediately. Serve warm.

CHOCOLATE CRUMB CAKE

2 cupfuls flour (all-purpose) . . . 1 cupful granulated sugar . . . ¼ teaspoonful salt . . . ½ teaspoonful baking powder . . . 1½ teaspoonfuls baking soda . . . ¼ cupful butter . . . 1 egg . . . ¾ cupful milk . . . ½ cupful (5½-ounce can) Hershey's Chocolate Flavored Syrup.

Mix flour and sugar and take out ½ cupful of "crumbs" and set aside. Add salt, baking powder and baking soda to remaining flour mixture. Blend in butter, egg, milk and chocolate syrup. Beat well; pour into a shallow well-greased pan (9 × 9 × 1¾-inch). Scatter reserved crumbs over top of cake, and bake in a moderate oven (350 degrees) 30 to 35 minutes. This cake should be served hot for luncheon or supper.

CHICAGO FUDGE CAKE

½ cupful butter . . . 2 cupfuls brown sugar, packed . . . 2 egg yolks . . . 1 teaspoonful vanilla . . . 4 squares Hershey's Baking Chocolate . . . ½ cupful hot water . . . 2½ cupfuls sifted cake flour . . . 1 teaspoonful baking soda . . . ½ teaspoonful salt . . . ½ cupful sour milk . . . 2 egg whites . . . ¼ teaspoonful cinnamon . . . ½ cupful raisins . . . ¼ cupful chopped nutmeats.

Cream the butter and brown sugar, and add the egg yolks and vanilla; beat well. Melt the baking chocolate over simmering water, and add to the creamed mixture. Rinse the chocolate pan with the hot water and add to the chocolate mixture. Then beat in the flour, sifted with the baking soda and salt, alternately with the sour milk. Beat the egg whites until stiff, and fold into the chocolate batter. Reserve 1½ cupfuls batter. Pour remaining batter into 2 greased and floured 8-inch layer pans. Stir cinnamon, raisins and nuts into reserved batter and pour into a greased and floured 8-inch layer pan. Bake in a moderate oven (350 degrees) for about 30 minutes. When baked, ice the cake all over with Fluffy Vanilla Icing (page 35) and before this is dry sprinkle with Hershey's Milk Chocolate Bar, finely grated.

Left to right:
Old-Fashioned Cocoa Mint Cake;
Hershey's Special Cake;
Chocolate Crumb Cake

COCOA POTATO CAKE

½ cupful butter . . . 2 cupfuls granulated sugar . . . 3 egg yolks . . . ½ teaspoonful vanilla . . . dash of cinnamon . . . 1 cupful hot mashed potatoes . . . ½ cupful Hershey's Cocoa . . . 2 cupfuls flour (all-purpose) . . . 2 teaspoonfuls baking powder . . . ½ cupful milk . . . ½ cupful chopped nuts . . . 3 egg whites.

Cream the butter and sugar together till very light. Add the egg yolks, one at a time, beating the mixture well after each has been added. Blend in the vanilla and cinnamon, and gradually add the mashed potatoes. Sift the cocoa, flour and baking powder together; add alternately with the milk to the creamed mixture. Stir in nuts. Beat egg whites until stiff peaks form, and fold into the chocolate batter. Pour into greased and floured pan (13 × 9 × 2-inch). Bake in a moderate oven (350 degrees) 30 to 35 minutes. Ice with Chocolate Nut Icing (page 32).

MARBLE CAKE

¾ cupful butter . . . 2 cupfuls granulated sugar . . . 1 teaspoonful vanilla . . . 2½ cupfuls cake flour . . . 2½ teaspoonfuls baking powder . . . 1 cupful milk . . . 5 egg whites, stiffly beaten . . . 2 squares Hershey's Baking Chocolate, melted.

Cream the butter well, adding sugar gradually, then add the vanilla and cream all together thoroughly. Sift the flour with the baking powder twice. Add alternately with the milk to the other ingredients. Beat hard, then fold in the egg whites. Remove about 1 cupful of the batter to a second bowl and to it add the melted baking chocolate. Arrange the white batter in a well-greased and floured loaf cake pan (13 × 9 × 2-inch) occasionally dropping in a spoonful of the chocolate batter. Stir just a little to produce a streaky effect. Bake in a moderate oven (350 degrees) for 35 to 40 minutes. Ice with Vanilla Butter Icing (page 30) and pour Chocolate Glaze (page 37) over it by spoonfuls, streaking a little to resemble marble.

RED DEVIL'S FOOD CAKE

½ cupful shortening . . . 1¼ cupfuls granulated sugar . . .
2 eggs, unbeaten . . . 1 cupful boiling water . . . ½ cupful.
Hershey's Cocoa . . . 1¾ cupfuls cake flour or 1½ cupfuls
flour (all-purpose) . . . 1 teaspoonful baking soda . . .
1 teaspoonful salt . . . 1 teaspoonful vanilla.

Cream shortening and sugar; add eggs, one at a time, beating well after each addition. Then add ingredients as called for and, after adding them all without stirring, beat vigorously until smooth. Turn into 2 greased and floured 8-inch layer pans. Bake in moderate oven (350 degrees) 30 to 35 minutes or until done.

COFFEE CHOCOLATE CAKE

4 squares Hershey's Baking Chocolate . . . 2 egg yolks . . .
1 cupful sour milk . . . ½ cupful butter . . . 2 cupfuls brown
sugar, packed . . . 1 teaspoonful vanilla . . . 3½ cupfuls flour
(all-purpose) . . . 1 teaspoonful baking soda . . . 1 teaspoonful
baking powder . . . ½ teaspoonful salt . . . 1 cupful clear
black coffee.

Melt the baking chocolate over simmering water; add the egg yolks, beaten with the milk, and cook till thick. Then cool. Cream the butter and sugar together, add the vanilla. Sift together the flour, baking soda, baking powder and salt, and add alternately with the coffee to the creamed mixture. Whip in the chocolate mixture and beat well. Pour into 2 greased and floured 9-inch cake layer pans, and bake in a moderate oven (350 degrees) 30 to 35 minutes. When cool, split each layer in half and fill with Chocolate Butter Filling (page 34) and ice with Chocolate Butter Icing (page 34).

OLD-FASHIONED CHOCOLATE CAKE

3 squares Hershey's Baking Chocolate . . . 5 tablespoonfuls
hot water . . . ½ cupful butter . . . 1½ cupfuls granulated sugar
. . . 4 eggs, separated . . . 1¾ cupfuls sifted cake flour . . .
2 teaspoonfuls baking powder . . . ½ teaspoonful salt . . .
½ cupful milk . . . 1 teaspoonful vanilla.

Melt the baking chocolate, cut into small pieces, with
the hot water in top of double boiler over simmering
water. Cream the butter and sugar together well; add the
egg yolks, well-beaten, and whip thoroughly. Then add
the melted chocolate mixture, slightly cooled, the flour
sifted with the baking powder and salt, and the milk.
Fold in the stiffly whipped egg whites and vanilla. Pour
into a well-greased and floured pan (13 × 9 × 2-inch).
Bake in a moderate oven (350 degrees) 40 to 45 minutes
or until done.

THREE LAYER GOLD CAKE
(Illustrated on cover)

1½ cupfuls granulated sugar . . . 1 cupful 4X sugar
(confectioners') . . . ½ cupful shortening . . . ½ cupful
butter . . . 5 egg yolks . . . 3 cupfuls sifted flour (all-purpose)
. . . 3 teaspoonfuls baking powder . . . ½ teaspoonful salt
. . . 1¼ cupfuls milk . . . 1 teaspoonful vanilla . . . 5 egg
whites.

Sift the granulated sugar and confectioners' sugar together into a large bowl. Cream well with shortening and
butter. Add the egg yolks and beat well. Sift together the
flour, baking powder and salt and add alternately with
the milk and vanilla to the creamed mixture. Beat the
egg whites until stiff and fold into the batter. Pour into
3 greased and floured 9-inch cake pans, and bake in a
moderate oven (350 degrees) for 35 to 40 minutes. Frost
with Three Layer Chocolate Icing (page 31).

DEVILS' DELIGHT CAKE

4 squares Hershey's Baking Chocolate, melted . . . ⅔ cupful
brown sugar, packed . . . 1 cupful milk . . . 1 egg yolk . . .
⅓ cupful butter . . . ½ cupful brown sugar, packed . . .
2 egg yolks . . . 2 cupfuls sifted cake flour . . . ¼ teaspoonful
salt . . . 1 teaspoonful baking soda . . . ½ cupful milk . . .
1 teaspoonful vanilla . . . 3 egg whites . . . ½ cupful brown
sugar, packed.

Combine melted baking chocolate with ⅔ cupful brown
sugar, 1 cupful milk and 1 beaten egg yolk, and stir
over simmering water until well blended. Cool slightly.
Cream butter, then add ½ cupful brown sugar gradually,
while beating constantly. Add 2 egg yolks, well-beaten.
Sift flour, salt and baking soda 3 times, and add to
creamed mixture alternately with ½ cupful milk, beating
thoroughly. Add chocolate mixture and vanilla, and beat.
Beat egg whites until foamy; gradually add ½ cupful
brown sugar and beat until stiff. Fold into batter. Pour
into 2 buttered and floured 9-inch round cake pans. Bake
in a moderate oven (350 degrees) for 35 minutes. Spread
layers and top with any favorite frosting, and cover
with thinly sliced oranges sprinkled with minced nutmeats and minced citron or candied ginger.

SIMPLE COCOA LAYER CAKE

½ cupful butter . . . 1¼ cupfuls granulated sugar . . . 1
teaspoonful vanilla . . . 2 egg yolks . . . 2 cupfuls flour (all-
purpose) . . . ¼ teaspoonful salt . . . ½ teaspoonful baking
soda . . . 1½ teaspoonfuls baking powder . . . ½ cupful
Hershey's Cocoa . . . 1¼ cupfuls milk . . . 2 egg whites.

Cream butter, sugar and vanilla, and add the well-
beaten egg yolks. Sift the flour, salt, baking soda, baking
powder and cocoa together. Add alternately with the
milk to the creamed mixture. Beat the egg whites until
stiff, and fold into the chocolate batter. Pour into 2
greased and floured 8-inch cake pans, and bake in a
moderate oven (350 degrees) 30 to 35 minutes. Put together and ice with Busy Day Cocoa Icing (page 35).

CHOCOLATE TOWN SYRUP CUPCAKES

½ cupful butter . . . 1 cupful granulated sugar . . . 1 teaspoonful vanilla . . . 4 eggs . . . 1¼ cupfuls flour (all-purpose) . . . ¾ teaspoonful baking soda . . . 1½ cupfuls (1-pound can) Hershey's Chocolate Flavored Syrup.

Cream the butter, sugar and vanilla until light and fluffy. Add the eggs, one at a time, beating well after each addition. Combine the flour and baking soda, and add alternately with the chocolate syrup to the creamed mixture. Pour the batter into paper-lined muffin cups, filling each ½ full. Bake in a moderate oven (375 degrees) for 20 to 25 minutes.
Yield: About 30 cupcakes.

CHOCOLATE ICEBERG CUPCAKES

½ cupful butter . . . 1 cupful fine sugar (superfine) . . . 2 egg yolks . . . 3 squares Hershey's Baking Chocolate, melted . . . 2 cupfuls sifted cake flour . . . ¾ teaspoonful baking soda . . . 1½ teaspoonfuls baking powder . . . ¼ teaspoonful salt . . . ⅔ cupful milk . . . 1 teaspoonful vanilla . . . 2 egg whites, beaten stiff . . . shredded cocoanut.

Cream butter and sugar together until light. Add egg yolks and beat. Blend in melted baking chocolate. Sift flour, baking soda, baking powder and salt together 3 times. Add flour mixture alternately with milk to creamed mixture, and beat thoroughly. Add vanilla. Fold in stiffly whipped whites. Pour into muffin tins which have been lined with paper baking cups, filling each ½ full. Bake in a moderate oven (350 degrees) 15 to 20 minutes. Spread cupcakes with Vanilla Butter Icing (page 30). Let frosting be rough and uneven, and sprinkle cupcakes with shredded cocoanut, chopped into short lengths, so that cupcakes resemble a frosty snow-covered iceberg.
Yield: About 30 cupcakes.

Icings & Sauces

Chocolate Glaze (page 37)

VANILLA BUTTER ICING

3 tablespoonfuls butter . . . 1½ cupfuls 4X sugar
(confectioners') . . . 1½ teaspoonfuls vanilla . . . 1 tablespoonful
milk . . . 4 drops red food coloring*

Beat butter and sugar; stir in vanilla and milk. Beat
until icing is smooth and of spreading consistency.
Yield: 1 cupful icing or enough for one 8- or 9-inch cake layer.
Pink Butter Icing

AUNT JESSIE'S CHOCOLATE ICING
(Uncooked)

¼ cupful butter . . . 1 ½ cupfuls 4X sugar (confectioners') . . .
2 egg yolks . . . about 2 tablespoonfuls milk or light cream . . .
1 teaspoonful vanilla . . . 2 squares Hershey's Baking
Chocolate, melted . . . ⅛ teaspoonful salt.

Cream butter; add sugar gradually, while beating constantly. Add egg yolks, milk or cream and vanilla. Add
melted baking chocolate and salt, and beat thoroughly.
Beat 3 to 5 minutes or until of right consistency to spread.
(This is a medium-dark icing that does not dry out even
when several days old.)
*Yield: 1⅔ cupfuls icing or enough for an 8- or 9-inch layer
cake.*

CHOCOLATE BUTTER ICING
(Uncooked)

¼ cupful butter . . . 2 cupfuls 4X sugar (confectioners') . . .
2 squares Hershey's Baking Chocolate, melted . . . 1 teaspoonful vanilla . . . about 2 tablespoonfuls milk or light cream.

Cream butter; add sugar gradually, while beating constantly. Add melted baking chocolate, then add vanilla.
Thin with milk or cream until of right consistency to
spread. Spread on warm cake. (This gives a rich icing of
medium color and decidedly fudge-like consistency.)
*Yield: 1⅓ cupfuls icing or enough for an 8- or 9-inch layer
cake.*

THREE LAYER CHOCOLATE ICING

5 squares Hershey's Baking Chocolate . . . 1½ cupfuls butter
. . . 3 egg yolks . . . 2 teaspoonfuls vanilla . . . 2 cupfuls
4X sugar (confectioners').

Melt the baking chocolate in top of double boiler over
simmering water. Cream the butter, egg yolks and vanilla
and slowly add baking chocolate. Add sugar to make of
proper consistency for spreading. *Yield: 2½ cupfuls icing or
enough for a three-layer 8- or 9-inch cake.*

CREOLE ICING

1 tablespoonful softened butter . . . ¼ cupful clear black
coffee . . . 3 tablespoonfuls Hershey's Cocoa . . . pinch of
cinnamon . . . 3¼ cupfuls 4X sugar (confectioners').

Combine butter, coffee, cocoa and cinnamon. Gradually
add sugar, beating to spreading consistency.
Yield: 1½ cupfuls icing or enough for an 8- or 9-inch layer cake.

MOCHA COCOA FROSTING

⅓ cupful butter . . . ½ teaspoonful vanilla . . . 3 cupfuls
4X sugar (confectioners') . . . ½ cupful Hershey's Cocoa . . .
¼ teaspoonful salt . . . about ⅓ cupful black coffee.

Cream butter thoroughly; add vanilla. Sift sugar, cocoa
and salt together. Add alternately with coffee to butter,
beating to spreading consistency. Spread on warm cake.
Yield: 1¾ cupfuls icing or enough for an 8- or 9-inch layer cake.

BITTER CHOCOLATE BUTTER ICING

½ cupful butter . . . 2 cupfuls 4X sugar (confectioners') . . .
2 tablespoonfuls light cream . . . 4 squares Hershey's Baking
Chocolate, melted.

Cream butter and sugar together; add cream and beat
well. Gradually add melted baking chocolate, and beat
thoroughly to reach spreading consistency. (Additional
cream may be needed.)
Yield: 2 cupfuls icing or enough for an 8- or 9-inch layer cake.

CHOCOLATE NUT ICING

¼ cupful Hershey's Cocoa . . . 6 tablespoonfuls boiling water
. . . ½ teaspoonful vanilla . . . 3 cupfuls 4X sugar
(confectioners') . . . ½ cupful chopped nuts.

Combine the cocoa and boiling water; add vanilla and sugar gradually. Beat until mixture reaches spreading consistency. (Additional boiling water may be needed.) Stir in nuts.
Yield: 1 cupful icing or enough for a 13 × 9 × 2-inch loaf cake.

FLUFFY CHOCOLATE ICING

1 cupful granulated sugar . . . 1 cupful water . . . pinch cream
of tartar . . . 2 egg whites . . . ¼ cupful Hershey's Cocoa . . .
½ teaspoonful vanilla.

Dissolve the sugar in the water, and add the cream of tartar. Boil to the soft-ball stage. (A small amount of mixture forms a soft ball when dropped into cold water, 234° F.) Beat egg whites until very stiff, then pour syrup in thin stream over them, beating all the time. Continue to beat until frosting is cool and of right consistency to spread, about 10 minutes. Carefully fold in cocoa and vanilla.
Yield: About 2½ cupfuls icing or enough for an 8- or 9-inch layer cake.

COCOA PEPPERMINT ICING

½ cupful butter . . . ½ cupful Hershey's Cocoa . . . 3⅔ cupfuls
(1-pound box) 4X sugar (confectioners') . . . 7 tablespoonfuls
milk . . . 1 teaspoonful vanilla . . . 1 tablespoonful crushed
peppermint candy.

Melt the butter in a saucepan; add the cocoa and heat 1 minute or until smooth, stirring constantly. Alternately add sugar and milk, beating to spreading consistency. Blend in vanilla and peppermint candy.
Yield: About 2¼ cupfuls icing or enough for an 8- or 9-inch layer cake.

Top to bottom:
Chocolate Nut Icing;
Fluffy Chocolate Icing;
Cocoa Peppermint Icing

CHOCOLATE BUTTER FILLING

5 tablespoonfuls butter . . . 1 ⅔ cupfuls 4X sugar (confectioners') . . . 2 squares Hershey's Baking Chocolate, melted . . . 1 tablespoonful water . . . ½ teaspoonful vanilla . . . ⅓ cupful heavy cream, whipped . . . ¼ cupful chopped nutmeats . . . ¼ cupful chopped maraschino cherries, drained.

Cream the butter and sugar, then add the melted baking chocolate, water and vanilla, and cream all well. Then fold in the whipped cream and the nuts and cherries. Spread torte-style between layers of chocolate or white cake after they have cooled.
Yield: About 1 cupful filling.

CHOCOLATE BUTTER ICING

3 squares Hershey's Baking Chocolate . . . 6 tablespoonfuls butter . . . 2 egg yolks . . . 1 teaspoonful vanilla . . . 1 cupful 4X sugar (confectioners').

Melt the baking chocolate in top of double boiler over simmering water. Cream the butter, egg yolks and vanilla, and slowly add melted baking chocolate. Add sugar to make of proper consistency for spreading.
Yield: 1¼ cupfuls icing or enough for an 8- or 9-inch layer cake.

MOCHA ICING

5 tablespoonfuls butter . . . 1 egg yolk . . . 3 tablespoonfuls Hershey's Cocoa . . . 2½ cupfuls 4X sugar (confectioners') . . . 3 tablespoonfuls strong black coffee (2 teaspoonfuls instant coffee and 3 tablespoonfuls hot water) . . . 1 teaspoonful vanilla.

Cream the butter, and add the egg yolk. Add the cocoa. Add sugar gradually to the butter mixture, alternating with the hot coffee. Cream well and flavor with vanilla. Add more sugar if necessary.
Yield: 1½ cupfuls icing or enough for an 8- or 9-inch layer cake.

BUSY DAY COCOA ICING

6 tablespoonfuls boiling water . . . ¼ cupful butter . . .
2 teaspoonfuls vanilla . . . ½ cupful Hershey's Cocoa . . .
3 cupfuls 4X sugar (confectioners').

Add boiling water to butter. Add vanilla and cocoa.
Beat and, when well blended, add sugar. Beat until smooth
and creamy adding additional liquid, if necessary, until
of right consistency to spread. Spread on warm cake.
(This is a good inexpensive and quick chocolate icing
with dark chocolate color. It keeps well for several days
without hardening.)
*Yield: About 2 cupfuls icing or enough to generously ice an 8-
or 9-inch layer cake.*

FLUFFY VANILLA ICING

1 cupful granulated sugar . . . 1 cupful water . . . pinch cream
of tartar . . . 2 egg whites . . . ½ teaspoonful vanilla.

Dissolve the sugar in the water, and add the cream of
tartar. Boil to the soft-ball stage (234° F.). Beat egg whites
until very stiff, then pour syrup over them, beating all
the time. Add the vanilla, and continue to beat until
frosting is cool and of right consistency to spread.
*Yield: About 3½ cupfuls icing or enough for three 8- or 9-inch
cake layers.*

ICING FOR CHOCOLATE MIDGETS

1 cupful 4X sugar (confectioners') . . . 3 tablespoonfuls
Hershey's Chocolate Flavored Syrup . . . ⅛ teaspoonful
vanilla . . . about 1 teaspoonful milk.

Mix the sugar and chocolate syrup together, and add
the vanilla. Add enough milk to make of proper spreading
consistency.
Yield: ¾ cupful icing or enough for an 8- or 9-inch cake layer.

MARSHMALLOW PEPPERMINT ICING

2 tablespoonfuls water . . . ½ cupful granulated sugar . . .
1 egg white, beaten stiff . . . ¾ cupful marshmallow whip . . .
few grains salt . . . ¼ teaspoonful peppermint extract . . .
few drops red food coloring.

Boil water and sugar together until it forms a soft ball in cold water (234° F.). Slowly pour hot syrup over beaten egg white, beating constantly. Add marshmallow whip, salt, extract and food coloring; beat until cool.
Yield: 2¼ cupfuls icing or enough for a 13 × 9 × 2-inch loaf cake.

CHOCOLATE SOUR CREAM FILLING AND ICING

2 cupfuls granulated sugar . . . 6 tablespoonfuls Hershey's Chocolate Flavored Syrup . . . ⅔ cupful sour cream (dairy) . . . 1 teaspoonful vanilla.

In a saucepan, combine the sugar and chocolate syrup. When well mixed, add the sour cream, and cook over medium heat to the soft-ball stage (234° F.). Remove from the fire; add vanilla and beat until thick enough to spread. Add nuts of any kind for variety.
Yield: 1½ cupfuls icing or enough for a 13 × 9 × 2-inch cake.

COCOA CREAM FILLING

2 tablespoonfuls butter . . . ⅓ cupful light cream . . .
½ cupful granulated sugar . . . ¼ cupful Hershey's Cocoa . . .
¼ teaspoonful vanilla.

Melt the butter over hot water. Add the cream, sugar and cocoa, and cook 1 minute. Cool, add vanilla and beat until of the right consistency to spread.
Yield: About ¾ cupful filling or enough for an 8- or 9-inch layer cake.

Left to right:
Cocoa Fudge Sauce;
Cocoa Chocolate Sauce;
Almond Bar Chocolate Sauce

CHOCOLATE GLAZE

1 square Hershey's Baking Chocolate . . . ½ teaspoonful butter.

Melt the baking chocolate and butter in top of double boiler over simmering water. Use as a top layer over white icings, orange icings, butterscotch or other icings.

CHOCOLATE GELATIN SAUCE

1 teaspoonful granulated gelatin (unflavored) . . .
2 tablespoonfuls cold water . . . 1 cupful granulated sugar . . .
⅓ cupful Hershey's Cocoa . . . ⅓ cupful water . . .
1 teaspoonful vanilla . . . ¼ teaspoonful salt.

Soak gelatin in cold water 5 minutes. Combine sugar, cocoa and ⅓ cupful water in saucepan. Blend, then boil 3 minutes, stirring constantly. Remove from heat and add softened gelatin to hot syrup. Stir until dissolved. Add vanilla and salt. Serve hot or cold over ice cream or desserts. If covered, it will keep well.
Yield: 1 cupful sauce.

COCOA CHOCOLATE SAUCE

¼ cupful butter . . . 2 squares Hershey's Baking Chocolate . . .
2 tablespoonfuls Hershey's Cocoa . . . ¾ cupful granulated
sugar . . . ½ cupful light cream . . . 1 teaspoonful vanilla.

Melt the butter and baking chocolate over simmering
water, then add the cocoa and sugar; cook for 5 minutes.
Stir in the cream and vanilla; simmer till blended. Serve.
Yield: 1 cupful sauce.

CHOCOLATE HARD SAUCE

2 tablespoonfuls butter . . . 3 tablespoonfuls Hershey's
Chocolate Flavored Syrup . . . ⅔ cupful 4X sugar
(confectioners') . . . few grains salt . . . ½ teaspoonful vanilla.

Cream butter; add chocolate syrup gradually. Blend in
sugar, salt and vanilla, beating constantly. Chill. Serve
over hot desserts.
Yield: ½ cupful sauce.

COCOA FUDGE SAUCE

¼ cupful Hershey's Cocoa . . . ¾ cupful granulated sugar . . .
½ teaspoonful salt . . . 1 tablespoonful cornstarch . . .
½ cupful light corn syrup . . . ½ cupful milk . . . 2
tablespoonfuls butter . . . 2 teaspoonfuls vanilla.

Combine dry ingredients in saucepan. Add corn syrup
and milk, and blend thoroughly. Bring to a boil, boil 5
minutes. Remove from heat; stir in butter and vanilla.
Cool, without stirring, until pan feels warm to hand. Serve.
Yield: 1½ cupfuls sauce.

ALMOND BAR CHOCOLATE SAUCE

4 Hershey's Milk Chocolate Bars with Almonds (1.05 ounces
each) . . . ¼ cupful hot water.

Melt milk chocolate bars in top of double boiler over
hot, not boiling, water. Add hot water, all at once, and
stir to blend until smooth. Serve as a hot topping.
Yield: ½ cupful sauce.

CHOCOLATE MARSHMALLOW SAUCE

2 cupfuls granulated sugar . . . 1 cupful boiling water . . .
¼ cupful Hershey's Cocoa . . . 1 teaspoonful vanilla . . .
½ cupful shredded fresh marshmallows (½ cupful miniature marshmallows).

Cook sugar and water in saucepan to 220° F. Remove from heat; stir in cocoa, vanilla and marshmallows until melted. Cool, without stirring, until bottom of pan just feels warm to hand. Beat to thicken and serve warm over ice cream.
Yield: 2 cupfuls sauce.

CLEAR COCOA SAUCE

¼ cupful Hershey's Cocoa . . . 1 tablespoonful cornstarch . . .
¾ cupful granulated sugar . . . dash of salt . . . 1¼ cupfuls hot water . . . 1 tablespoonful butter . . . 1 teaspoonful vanilla.

Mix together the cocoa, cornstarch, sugar and salt. Pour the hot water over the mixture, and cook over medium heat, stirring constantly, till clear, thick and smooth. Add the butter and vanilla, and serve hot with any desired pudding or ice cream.
Yield: 1¾ cupfuls sauce.

CHOCOLATE CARAMEL SAUCE

1 cupful brown sugar, packed . . . dash of salt . . .
3 tablespoonfuls water . . . ¼ cupful Hershey's Chocolate Flavored Syrup . . . 1 tablespoonful butter . . . 1 tablespoonful cornstarch . . . 1 cupful hot water . . . ½ teaspoonful vanilla.

Cook the sugar and salt with 3 tablespoonfuls water to a light caramel brown. Remove from heat; add chocolate syrup, then the butter and cornstarch, mixed to a paste, and the hot water. Cook over direct heat until thick (220° F.), about 15 minutes; add vanilla. Serve with cottage pudding or any hot dessert. This sauce is very nice with ice cream.
Yield: 1 cupful sauce.

Pies

Chocolate Chiffon Pie (page 42)

CHOCOLATE CHIFFON PIE

1 tablespoonful granulated gelatin (unflavored) . . .
3 tablespoonfuls cold water . . . 1 cupful (6-ounce package)
Hershey's Baking Chips . . . ½ cupful milk . . .
⅓ cupful granulated sugar . . . ½ teaspoonful salt . . .
¾ cupful milk . . . 3 egg yolks . . . 1 teaspoonful vanilla . . .
3 egg whites . . . ¼ teaspoonful cream of tartar . . .
⅓ cupful granulated sugar . . . 9-inch baked pie shell.

Soften the gelatin in the cold water. Melt baking pieces with ½ cupful milk in saucepan over low fire, stirring constantly, until pieces are melted and mixture is smooth. Remove from fire; stir in the ⅓ cupful sugar, salt, ¾ cupful milk, softened gelatin mixture and egg yolks, slightly beaten. Return to fire and cook, stirring constantly, until mixture thickens. Remove from fire and add vanilla. Pour into bowl and press waxed paper directly onto filling. Cool. Chill until mixture begins to thicken. Beat egg whites with cream of tartar until frothy. Gradually add ⅓ cupful sugar and beat until stiff peaks form. Carefully fold gelatin mixture into egg whites. Pour into baked pie shell. Chill. Just before serving, garnish with whipped cream if desired.

CHOCOLATE BROWNIE PIE

3 eggs . . . ⅓ cupful butter . . . 1½ cupfuls granulated sugar
. . . ¾ cupful sifted flour (all-purpose) . . . ½ teaspoonful salt
. . . 3 squares Hershey's Baking Chocolate, melted . . .
⅓ cupful milk . . . 1 teaspoonful vanilla . . . 1 cupful chopped nuts.

Beat the eggs until very light. Cream the butter, and add the sugar gradually, beating until light and fluffy. Sift the flour and the salt; set aside. Then add the cooled melted baking chocolate and the beaten eggs to creamed mixture. Add the flour mixture alternately with the milk to which the vanilla has been added. Then stir in the nuts. Pour mixture into a greased 9-inch pie pan. Bake in a moderate oven (375 degrees) for 45 to 50 minutes. Serve the pie topped with ice cream or whipped cream if desired.

Chocolate Butterscotch Pie

CHOCOLATE BUTTERSCOTCH PIE

¾ cupful brown sugar, packed . . . ⅓ cupful flour (all-purpose) . . . ½ teaspoonful salt . . . 2½ cupfuls milk . . . 6 tablespoonfuls Hershey's Chocolate Flavored Syrup . . . 2 egg yolks, well-beaten . . . 2 tablespoonfuls butter . . . ½ teaspoonful vanilla . . . 9-inch baked pie shell.

Thoroughly combine sugar, flour and salt. Stir in the milk, chocolate syrup and beaten egg yolks. Cook over medium heat until thick, stirring constantly. Remove from fire; blend in butter and vanilla. Pour into baked pie shell; cool. Chill in refrigerator. Serve with sweetened whipped cream if desired.

CHOCOLATE CREAM PIE

2½ cupfuls milk . . . 3 squares Hershey's Baking Chocolate, melted . . . 2 tablespoonfuls flour (all-purpose) . . . 3 tablespoonfuls cornstarch . . . 1 cupful granulated sugar . . . ½ teaspoonful salt . . . 4 egg yolks, slightly beaten . . . 2 tablespoonfuls butter . . . 1½ teaspoonfuls vanilla . . . 9-inch baked pie shell . . . 4 egg whites . . . ½ teaspoonful cream of tartar . . . ½ cupful granulated sugar.

Scald 2 cupfuls milk with melted baking chocolate in top of double boiler over simmering water, stirring until smooth. Sift flour, cornstarch, 1 cupful sugar and salt twice. Mix with remaining ½ cupful of milk. Add to chocolate mixture, stirring constantly, until thickened. Cook 10 minutes longer. Remove from fire; gradually add some of chocolate mixture to beaten egg yolks and return to double boiler. Cook 2 minutes longer, stirring occasionally. Remove from fire; add butter and vanilla. Pour into baked pie shell. Cover with meringue made by beating egg whites with cream of tartar until frothy. Gradually add ½ cupful sugar (a tablespoonful at a time), beating until stiff. Brown in hot oven (425 degrees) about 5 minutes. Cool to room temperature. Chill; serve cold.

CHOCOLATE RAISIN PIE

⅓ cupful Hershey's Baking Chips . . . 1½ cupfuls seedless raisins . . . 1 cupful light cream . . . ¼ cupful butter . . . 1 teaspoonful vanilla . . . ¾ cupful granulated sugar . . . 3 tablespoonfuls cornstarch . . . ⅛ teaspoonful salt . . . ⅛ teaspoonful cinnamon . . . 2 eggs . . . 9-inch unbaked pie shell.

Place baking pieces, raisins, cream and butter in a heavy saucepan. Stir over low fire until baking pieces and butter are melted. Remove from fire and stir in vanilla. Mix together sugar, cornstarch, salt and cinnamon. Stir into raisin mixture. Beat eggs well with rotary beater until foamy and stir in. Pour into unbaked pie shell, spreading raisins evenly over bottom. Bake in moderate oven (375 degrees) for 40 to 45 minutes or until set. Cool. Top with whipped cream if desired.

Top to bottom:
Cocoa Cream Pie;
Chocolate Cream Pie;
Chocolate Raisin Pie

COCOA CREAM PIE

¼ cupful Hershey's Cocoa . . . ¾ cupful granulated sugar . . . 3 tablespoonfuls cornstarch . . . ¼ teaspoonful salt . . . 2 cupfuls milk . . . 2 egg yolks . . . 1 tablespoonful butter . . . 1 teaspoonful vanilla . . . 8-inch baked pie shell . . . 2 egg whites . . . ¼ teaspoonful cream of tartar . . . ¼ cupful granulated sugar . . . ½ teaspoonful vanilla.

Mix together cocoa, ¾ cupful sugar, cornstarch and salt in a saucepan. Gradually stir in milk, mixing well until smooth. Cook over medium heat until filling thickens, stirring constantly. Boil 1 minute and remove from heat. Slowly stir about half the chocolate mixture into slightly beaten egg yolks. Then blend into hot mixture in saucepan. Boil 1 minute more, stirring constantly. Remove from heat and blend in butter and vanilla. Pour into baked pie shell, and cover with a meringue made by beating the egg whites with cream of tartar until foamy. Add 4 tablespoonfuls of sugar gradually and beat until stiff peaks hold. Flavor with ½ teaspoonful vanilla. Pile onto pie and brown in hot oven (400 degrees) 8 to 10 minutes.

TRIPLE CHOCOLATE PIE

1 tablespoonful granulated gelatin (unflavored) . . . ⅔ cupful granulated sugar . . . ¼ teaspoonful salt . . . 1 cupful milk . . . 3 egg yolks, beaten . . . 3 squares Hershey's Baking Chocolate . . . 1 teaspoonful vanilla . . . 3 egg whites . . . ¼ teaspoonful cream of tartar . . . ¼ cupful granulated sugar . . . 1 cupful whipping cream, whipped . . . 9-inch baked pie shell.

Mix together gelatin, ⅔ cupful sugar and salt in a saucepan, and then blend in the milk and beaten egg yolks; add the baking chocolate. Heat slowly, stirring constantly, over medium fire until chocolate is melted and the mixture thickens slightly. Pour into a large bowl and add vanilla; stir until smooth and blended. Cool. Chill until mixture mounds.

Beat the egg whites with cream of tartar until foamy in a small bowl. Gradually add the ¼ cupful sugar and beat until the meringue stands in stiff peaks. Beat the cooled chocolate mixture until smooth, then fold in the meringue and then fold in half the whipped cream. Pour into baked pie shell. Chill several hours or until firm enough to cut. Garnish with remaining whipped cream.

MARBLE-TOP CHOCOLATE PIE

½ cupful granulated sugar . . . 1 tablespoonful granulated gelatin (unflavored) : . . dash of salt . . . 1 cupful milk . . . 2 egg yolks, beaten . . . 1 cupful (6-ounce package) Hershey's Baking Chips . . . 1 teaspoonful vanilla . . . 2 egg whites . . . ¼ cupful granulated sugar . . . 1 cupful heavy cream . . . ½ teaspoonful vanilla . . . 2 tablespoonfuls 4X sugar (confectioners') . . . 9-inch baked pie shell or crumb crust.

In a heavy saucepan, combine the ½ cupful granulated sugar, the gelatin and salt. Stir in the milk and egg yolks. Cook and stir over medium fire till mixture just begins to boil. Do not boil. Remove from fire, and add baking pieces, then stir until melted. Add the vanilla. Cool and then chill mixture till set. Beat egg whites till foamy, then gradually add the ¼ cupful granulated sugar, beating till stiff peaks form. Whip the cream till stiff, then add the vanilla and 4X sugar and blend. Beat the chilled gelatin mixture until smooth. Then (on low speed of mixer) fold the stiffly beaten whites into the gelatin mixture. Alternately layer chiffon mixture and whipped cream into a 9-inch baked pie shell or crumb crust. Then swirl the knife through the pie to give it a marbled effect. Chill till firm.

CHOCOLATE PIE SHELL

⅓ cupful shortening . . . 1 cupful sifted flour (all-purpose) . . . ¼ teaspoonful salt . . . 1 Hershey's Special Dark Bar (1.05 ounces), grated . . . 3 to 4 tablespoonfuls water.

Cut the shortening into flour and salt in a bowl. Stir in semi-sweet chocolate and then sprinkle water over. Mix lightly, just until dough holds together. Roll out and line a 9-inch pie plate; flute edges. Bake in a hot oven (450 degrees) for about 12 minutes.

Desserts

Old-Fashioned Chocolate Ice Cream (page 50)

OLD-FASHIONED CHOCOLATE
ICE CREAM

2 tablespoonfuls granulated gelatin (unflavored) . . . ½ cupful cold water . . . 1 cupful rich milk . . . 1½ cupfuls (1-pound can) Hershey's Chocolate Flavored Syrup . . . ¾ cupful granulated sugar . . . few grains salt . . . 1 pint light cream . . . 1 pint heavy cream . . . 2 tablespoonfuls vanilla.

Allow the gelatin to soak in the water in a saucepan for 5 minutes. Add the milk and heat, stirring until the gelatin is dissolved. Remove from heat and add the chocolate syrup, sugar and salt. Cool. Add the creams and the vanilla. Freeze in a crank freezer. (See freezing instructions with the Chocolate Custard Ice Cream, opposite.)
Yield: 4 quarts ice cream.
Variation: Dissolve ¼ cupful crushed peppermint candy with the gelatin or add ¼ teaspoonful peppermint extract when adding vanilla.

CHOCOLATE ICE CREAM

2 squares Hershey's Baking Chocolate . . . 1 cupful sweetened condensed milk . . . 1 cupful water . . . ¼ teaspoonful vanilla . . . 1 cupful heavy cream, whipped.

Melt the baking chocolate in a double boiler over simmering water. Add the condensed milk, and stir over boiling water for 5 minutes. Add the water and blend well. Cool, then add vanilla. Fold in stiffly whipped cream. Pour into a chilled pan (8 × 8 × 2-inch) and place in freezer and freeze. Serve individually with fancy wafers.
Yield: 6 servings.

CHOCOLATE CUSTARD ICE CREAM

2 cupfuls granulated sugar . . . ¼ cupful flour (all-purpose)
. . . ⅛ teaspoonful salt . . . 2 cupfuls rich milk . . . 4 squares
Hershey's Baking Chocolate . . . 2 eggs . . . 4 cupfuls light
cream . . . 2 tablespoonfuls vanilla.

Combine the sugar, flour and salt in top of a double
boiler. Add the milk gradually and then add the baking
chocolate. Cook over the boiling water, stirring constantly, until thick, then cook 10 minutes longer, stirring
occasionally. Stir a small amount of cooked mixture into
slightly beaten eggs. Return to the double boiler and
cook 3 minutes longer. Cool. Add the cream and the
vanilla. Chill mixture, then freeze.

To freeze, fill the chilled container ⅔ full with ice
cream mixture. Cover tightly and set into freezer tub.
(For an electric freezer, follow manufacturer's directions.)
Fill tub with alternate 3-inch layers of crushed ice and
1 part rock salt. Turn the handle slowly for 5 minutes.
Turn rapidly until the handle becomes difficult to turn
(about 15 minutes). Remove the dasher and pack down
ice cream and cover with waxed paper. Again put the
lid on top and fill opening for dasher with cork. Repack
freezer in ice using 4 parts crushed ice and 1 part rock
salt. Cover with paper or cloth. Let ripen 2 to 3 hours.
Yield: 4 quarts ice cream.

COCOA CREAM TAPIOCA

2¾ cupfuls milk . . . 3 tablespoonfuls granulated sugar . . .
¼ teaspoonful salt . . . 6 tablespoonfuls Hershey's Chocolate
Flavored Syrup . . . ¼ cupful quick-cooking tapioca . . .
½ teaspoonful vanilla . . . heavy cream.

Bring milk to boiling point; add sugar, salt, chocolate
syrup and stir in tapioca. Cook over boiling water till
clear and well done. Add vanilla; cool and pour into
serving dishes and press waxed paper directly onto surface
of pudding. Chill and top with heavy cream, sweetened
and whipped.
Yield: 8 to 10 servings.

CHOCOLATE CORNSTARCH PUDDING

3 squares Hershey's Baking Chocolate . . . 3 cupfuls rich milk . . . 1 cupful granulated sugar . . . ¼ cupful cornstarch . . . ¼ teaspoonful salt . . . 1 tablespoonful butter . . . 1 teaspoonful vanilla.

Melt baking chocolate in double boiler over simmering water, and add milk. Stir until well blended. Combine together the sugar, cornstarch and salt, and add a small amount of hot chocolate mixture, stirring vigorously. Return to double boiler and cook until thickened, stirring constantly. Cook 20 minutes longer. Add butter and vanilla. Spoon into serving dishes and press waxed paper directly onto surface of pudding. Cool and chill. Serve with sweetened whipped cream if desired.
Yield: 6 servings.

CHOCOLATE BREAD PUDDING

1 cupful (6-ounce package) Hershey's Baking Chips . . . 3 cupfuls milk . . . ½ teaspoonful salt . . . 4 egg yolks . . . ¾ cupful granulated sugar . . . 1 teaspoonful vanilla . . . 8 slices dry bread . . . ½ cupful broken nuts . . . 3 egg whites . . . ¼ teaspoonful cream of tartar . . . ½ cupful granulated sugar.

Melt the baking pieces in 1 cupful milk over medium heat. Stir in the remaining 2 cupfuls milk and reserve. Combine together the salt, egg yolks, ¾ cupful granulated sugar and vanilla, and stir in reserved mixture. Trim crusts from bread and cut slices into ½-inch cubes. Place cubes into 1½-quart casserole. Pour custard mixture over the bread cubes, being sure that all the cubes are saturated, and then blend in the nuts. Set the casserole in pan of hot water. Then bake in a moderate oven (350 degrees) for 1 hour. Beat the egg whites and the cream of tartar until frothy. Gradually add the ½ cupful granulated sugar, and beat until the meringue is stiff. Spread meringue on casserole, brown delicately in the oven. Serve warm or cold.
Yield: 14 servings.

ANGEL CHOCOLATE PARFAIT

½ teaspoonful granulated gelatin (unflavored) . . .
2 tablespoonfuls cold water . . . 1 cupful water . . . 1 cupful
granulated sugar . . . 2 egg whites, beaten stiff . . .
¼ teaspoonful salt . . . 2 squares Hershey's Baking Chocolate,
melted . . . 1 teaspoonful vanilla or ½ teaspoonful almond
extract . . . 1 cupful heavy cream, whipped.

Soak gelatin in the cold water for 5 minutes. Boil the
1 cupful of water with 1 cupful sugar until it spins a
thread (240° F.). Add dissolved gelatin. Pour syrup in a
fine stream over egg whites, stiffly whipped with the
salt. Keep beating continuously, while adding melted
baking chocolate, and add flavoring. Fold in stiffly whipped
cream. Pour into chilled pan (8 × 8 × 2-inch) and freeze
without stirring. Serve in tall parfait glasses and garnish
with whipped cream and cherry.
Yield: 4 servings.

CHOCOLATE FLOATING ISLANDS

1 pint milk . . . 1 square Hershey's Baking Chocolate, melted
. . . ½ cupful granulated sugar . . . ⅛ teaspoonful salt . . .
4 egg yolks . . . ½ teaspoonful vanilla . . . 3 egg whites . . .
¼ teaspoonful cream of tartar . . . ¼ cupful granulated sugar.

Scald the milk in a double boiler; add the melted baking chocolate and blend. Combine the ½ cupful sugar and salt, and stir into the milk. Gradually stir half of the chocolate mixture into the slightly beaten egg yolks. Return to the double boiler and cook over simmering water, stirring constantly until thick enough to mask the spoon. Add the vanilla, then pour into a serving casserole dish. Cool, and then chill.

For the Floating Islands, beat the whites of the eggs and the cream of tartar until very stiff, adding 4 tablespoonfuls of sugar. Drop the egg whites onto the custard. Place the custard dish in a pan of ice water and put the whole into a hot oven (425 degrees) just long enough to brown the tips of the meringue. Serve immediately.
Yield: 10 servings.

CHOCOLATE TRIFLE

Prepare the chocolate custard as for Chocolate Floating Islands (above) and cool. Line a glass serving dish with lady fingers, spread these with a thin layer of pineapple or orange marmalade and cover with a second layer of lady fingers. Pour the custard in carefully and leave for an hour, then cover the top of the custard with meringue (made from the 3 egg whites, ¼ teaspoonful cream of tartar beaten until stiff, adding ¼ cupful granulated sugar; cover the top of trifle with meringue). Set serving dish in a pan of ice water and brown delicately in a hot oven (425 degrees) for a few minutes. Chill and serve.
Yield: 12 servings.

Left to right:
Angel Chocolate Parfait;
Chocolate Trifle;
Chocolate Floating Islands

STEAMED CHOCOLATE PUDDING

2 squares Hershey's Baking Chocolate . . . 1 egg . . . ¾ cupful granulated sugar . . . ½ cupful milk . . . 2 tablespoonfuls butter, melted . . . 1 cupful flour (all-purpose) . . . 1 tablespoonful baking powder . . . ¼ teaspoonful salt . . . ½ teaspoonful vanilla.

Melt the baking chocolate over simmering water. Beat the egg and sugar well; add other ingredients and melted baking chocolate. Turn into a well-greased mold and steam for 1½ hours. (Place rack in large saucepan and pour boiling water into pan up to level of rack. Place mold with pudding on rack. Cover saucepan and keep water boiling over low heat to steam pudding.) Serve with Chocolate Hard Sauce (page 38).
Yield: 14 servings.

BAKED CHOCOLATE RICE PUDDING

½ cupful regular rice . . . 1 cupful water . . . ⅔ cupful granulated sugar . . . 1 tablespoonful cornstarch . . . ⅓ cupful Hershey's Cocoa . . . dash of salt . . . 2½ cupfuls milk . . . 2 egg yolks . . . ½ cupful raisins . . . 2 egg whites . . . ¼ cupful granulated sugar.

Stir together the rice and water in a saucepan. Heat to boiling, stirring once or twice. Reduce heat and cover and simmer 14 minutes without removing the cover or stirring. All the water should be absorbed. Blend ⅔ cupful sugar, the cornstarch, cocoa and salt. Add the ½ cupful milk to mixture and stir to form a paste, then add remaining milk. Add beaten egg yolks and beat with a rotary beater. Stir in rice and raisins. Pour into ungreased 1½-quart casserole.

Place casserole in pan of very hot water. Bake in a moderate oven (350 degrees) for about 1½ hours, stirring occasionally, or until the pudding is creamy and most of the liquid is absorbed. Remove casserole from the oven but not from pan of hot water. Increase the oven temperature to a hot oven (400 degrees). Beat the egg whites until foamy. Beat in ¼ cupful sugar and continue beating until stiff and glossy. Spread on the pudding, and bake 8 to 10 minutes to brown meringue. Serve warm.
Yield: 12 servings.

CHOCOLATE BAVARIAN CREAM

1 tablespoonful granulated gelatin (unflavored) . . . ¼ cupful cold water . . . 2 squares Hershey's Baking Chocolate . . . 1 cupful granulated sugar . . . few grains salt . . . ½ cupful hot milk . . . 1 teaspoonful vanilla . . . 2 cupfuls heavy cream, whipped . . . about 24 "arrowroot" wafers or lady fingers.

Soak gelatin in the cold water. Melt the baking chocolate in a double boiler over simmering water. Add the sugar, salt and hot milk; blend. Add the gelatin to the hot mixture. Cool the chocolate mixture. Then beat mixture until spongy and light (about 2 minutes), and add the vanilla. Fold in the whipped cream. Line the bottom and sides of a fancy mold with round "arrowroot" wafers or ladyfingers. (Substitute strips of sponge cake for wafers, if desired.) Pour in cream mixture. Mold and chill. Garnish with sweetened whipped cream.
Yield: 12 servings.

CHOCOLATE-MARSHMALLOW CREAM ROLL

6 egg yolks . . . 6 tablespoonfuls Hershey's Cocoa . . . 1 heaping cupful 4X sugar (confectioners') . . . dash of salt . . . ½ cupful cake flour . . . 1 teaspoonful vanilla . . . 6 egg whites, stiffly beaten.

Beat the egg yolks until thick and lemon-colored, and add the cocoa, sugar, salt, flour and vanilla. (Mixture will be stiff.) Then fold in ¼ of the stiffly beaten egg whites; blend well. Fold in remaining egg whites and turn into a greased pan (15 × 9 × 2-inch) which has been lined with waxed paper. Bake in a moderate oven (350 degrees) 20 minutes. Turn out onto a damp towel, roll up and let rest 1 minute. Unroll and reroll without towel. Cool on rack covered with waxed paper. Fill with Marshmallow Peppermint Icing (page 36) and cover with ½ recipe Bitter Chocolate Butter Icing (page 31). If desired, garnish with flowers made by cutting marshmallows into very thin strips, using candied cherries as centers.
Yield: 12 servings.

CHOCOLATE MARSHMALLOW PUDDING

½ cupful (5½-ounce can) Hershey's Chocolate Flavored
Syrup . . . 3 cupfuls milk . . . ¼ cupful sugar . . . dash of salt
. . . 3 tablespoonfuls flour (all-purpose) . . . 1 egg . . .
1 teaspoonful vanilla . . . marshmallows.

Add the chocolate syrup to the milk and scald. Mix
together the sugar, salt, flour and well-beaten egg with a
little water to thin (about 2 tablespoonfuls), if necessary.
Pour about half of the scalded milk over the egg mixture,
return to pan and cook until mixture just begins to boil.
Remove from the fire and add vanilla. Pour into a baking
dish (about 1½-quart size); top with marshmallows and
brown delicately in hot oven (400 degrees). Chill and
serve cold.
Yield: 12 servings.

COCOA MERINGUE CAKE

½ cupful butter . . . ⅔ cupful granulated sugar . . . 4 eggs . . .
¼ cupful Hershey's Cocoa . . . 1 cupful flour (all-purpose) . . .
1½ teaspoonfuls baking powder . . . ½ cupful milk . . .
¼ teaspoonful cream of tartar . . . ½ cupful granulated sugar
. . . ½ teaspoonful vanilla . . . chopped pecans.

Put together like any cake, using only the egg yolks.
(Cream butter and ⅔ cupful sugar; add egg yolks and
blend well. Sift together the cocoa, flour and baking
powder, and add alternately with the milk.) Spread in 2
greased and floured 9-inch layer cake pans, and cover
each with a meringue made by whipping the whites of the
eggs and cream of tartar until frothy. Continue beating,
gradually adding ½ cupful granulated sugar, beating until
stiff. Flavor with the vanilla. Sprinkle a few chopped
pecan meats over the meringues, and bake the cakes in
a slow oven (325 degrees) for 30 minutes. Cool. Make
Cocoa Cream Filling (page 36) and put between the layers.

CHOCOLATE SYRUP MOUSSE

1 cupful Hershey's Chocolate Flavored Syrup . . . ⅓ cupful
sweetened condensed milk . . . 1 teaspoonful vanilla . . . few
grains salt . . . 2 cupfuls heavy cream, whipped . . . 2 egg
whites, stiffly whipped.

Combine together the chocolate syrup, condensed
milk, vanilla and salt, and blend well. Chill thoroughly.
Add whipped cream and whip until mixture is spongy
and light. Fold in stiffly beaten egg whites. Freeze in a
pan (8 × 8 × 2-inch). After mixture has frozen for 1
hour, scrape sides and stir. Finish freezing.
Yield: 8 servings.

MOCHA CHOCOLATE MARLOW

1½ squares Hershey's Baking Chocolate . . . ½ cupful strong
coffee . . . ¼ cupful granulated sugar . . . few grains salt . . .
1 cupful marshmallow whip . . . 1 cupful cream, whipped . . .
⅓ cupful chopped nuts.

Heat together over medium fire baking chocolate and
coffee until chocolate is melted. Add the sugar, salt and
marshmallow whip, then stir till blended. Cool and chill
till slightly thickened, carefully fold in stiffly whipped
cream and nuts. Pour into an 8 × 8 × 2-inch pan. Freeze
about 6 hours.
Yield: 8 servings.

Breads

Chocolate Chip Orange Muffins (page 62)

CHOCOLATE CHIP ORANGE MUFFINS

1½ cupfuls flour (all-purpose) . . . ½ cupful granulated sugar
. . . 2 teaspoonfuls baking powder . . . ½ teaspoonful salt . . .
1 egg . . . ½ cupful milk . . . ¼ cupful vegetable oil . . .
¾ cupful Hershey's Milk Chocolate Chips . . . 1½ to 2
teaspoonfuls grated orange peel.

Sift together the flour, the sugar, the baking powder
and the salt. Beat the egg and add to the flour mixture.
Then add the milk and the vegetable oil, stirring only to
moisten the flour. Mix in the milk chocolate pieces and
the orange peel. Fill greased muffin tins (2¾ inches in
diameter) ⅔ full. Bake in a hot oven (400 degrees) for
20 to 25 minutes.
Yield: 12 muffins.

ORANGE-COCOA
AFTERNOON TEA BISCUITS

1¾ cupfuls flour (all-purpose) . . . 4 teaspoonfuls baking
powder . . . ½ cupful Hershey's Cocoa . . . ½ teaspoonful salt
. . . ½ cupful granulated sugar . . . 3 tablespoonfuls butter . . .
¾ cupful milk . . . 24 pieces loaf sugar (sugar cubes) . . .
¼ cupful orange juice.

Sift all the dry ingredients together twice; work in the
butter with a knife and add the liquid gradually. Turn
out on a floured board and roll ¼ inch thick; cut in small
rounds (2½ inches in diameter). Place each biscuit in a
paper case, and press into the center a piece of a loaf
sugar which has been soaked in orange juice. Bake in a
hot oven (425 degrees) about 10 to 12 minutes. Serve hot.
Yield: 2 dozen biscuits.

SPICED COCOA DOUGHNUTS

2 cupfuls flour (all-purpose) . . . ½ cupful Hershey's Cocoa . . .
2½ teaspoonfuls baking powder . . . ½ teaspoonful baking
soda . . . ¼ teaspoonful salt . . . ¼ teaspoonful cinnamon . . .
¼ teaspoonful mace . . . 1½ tablespoonfuls softened butter
. . . ¾ cupful granulated sugar . . . 1 egg . . . ½ cupful milk.

Sift together the flour, cocoa, baking powder, baking
soda, salt and spices. Cream butter and sugar and beat
in egg well. Add dry ingredients alternately with milk
and mix well. Turn out on floured board and roll ¼ inch
thick; cut into small dainty rings (2½ inches in diameter).
Fry in deep fat (370° F.) for about 30 seconds. Drain on
paper; sprinkle lightly when cool with 4X sugar (confectioners') mixed with a little cinnamon.
Yield: About 2 dozen doughnuts.

RAISIN-NUT COCOA BREAD

2 yeast cakes (2 packages active dry yeast) . . . ½ cupful
lukewarm water . . . 1 cupful brown sugar, packed . . .
2 tablespoonfuls butter . . . 1 cupful nutmeats . . . 1 cupful
raisins or dates, cut in small pieces . . . ½ teaspoonful salt
. . . 2 cupfuls cooked cereal, lukewarm (oatmeal) . . . 6 to 6½
cupfuls flour (all-purpose) . . . ½ cupful Hershey's Cocoa.

Dissolve the yeast in lukewarm water 10 minutes. Add
the sugar, butter, nutmeats, raisins, salt and yeast mixture
to the lukewarm cereal. Sift 2 cupfuls of the flour and
the cocoa together. Add to the cereal mixture and beat
well. Add remaining flour. Place dough in a lightly greased
bowl and turn over to grease top. Cover with a cloth and
leave to rise until doubled in a warm place. Punch down,
make into 2 loaves and place in greased bread pans (9 × 5
× 2¾-inch). Let rise again in a warm place until doubled.
Bake in a moderate oven (375 degrees) 30 to 35 minutes.
Brush loaves with butter while still hot.
Yield: 2 loaves.

CHOCOLATE DESSERT WAFFLES

½ cupful butter . . . 2 squares Hershey's Baking Chocolate
. . . ¾ cupful granulated sugar . . . 1 teaspoonful vanilla . . .
2 eggs . . . 1½ cupfuls flour (all-purpose) . . . ½ teaspoonful
baking soda . . . 1 teaspoonful cream of tartar . . . ½ cupful
buttermilk . . . 1 cupful chopped nuts.

Melt butter and baking chocolate together in the top
part of a double boiler over simmering water. Add the
sugar and beat well. Stir in the vanilla. Add the eggs,
one at a time, and beat well after each addition. Combine the flour, baking soda and cream of tartar, and add
alternately with the buttermilk to the first mixture. Then
add the nuts and blend well.

If baked on a well-heated electric waffle iron, no greas-
ing will be required. If on an ordinary waffle iron, use
just 6 tablespoonfuls of the butter in the batter and grease
the heated waffle iron lightly with the remaining 2 tablespoonfuls of butter.

When first taken from the waffle iron, the waffle will
be soft, but will become crisp as it cools. These waffles
are delicious served hot from the waffle iron with vanilla
ice cream.

Yield: Twenty four 5-inch waffles.

CHOCOLATE TEA BREAD

¼ cupful butter . . . ⅔ cupful granulated sugar . . . 1 egg
. . . 2 cupfuls sifted cake flour . . . 1 teaspoonful baking
soda . . . ¾ teaspoonful salt . . . ⅓ cupful Hershey's Cocoa
. . . 1 teaspoonful cinnamon . . . 1 cupful buttermilk . . .
1 cupful raisins . . . ¾ cupful chopped walnuts.

Cream butter; add sugar, a small amount at a time,
creaming well after each addition. Add egg and beat well.
Mix and sift together the flour, baking soda, salt, cocoa
and cinnamon; add to creamed mixture alternately with
the buttermilk, beating until blended after each addition.
Stir in raisins and nuts. Turn into a greased bread pan
(9 × 5 × 2¾-inch). Bake in a moderate oven (350 degrees)
1 hour or until done. Cool on wire rack. Spread with
softened cream cheese if desired.

Left to right:
Chocolate Tea Bread;
Chocolate Dessert Waffles

Cookies

Cocoa Bread Crumb Cookies (page 74)

CAROL'S CHOCOLATE COCOANUT SQUARES

⅓ cupful butter . . . 1½ cupfuls brown sugar, packed . . . 2 eggs . . . 1 teaspoonful vanilla . . . 1 cupful flour (all-purpose) . . . 1¼ teaspoonfuls baking powder . . . ¼ cupful Hershey's Cocoa . . . ½ teaspoonful salt . . . ½ cupful milk . . . ½ cupful graham cracker crumbs, rolled fine . . . ½ cupful shredded cocoanut . . . ¾ cupful finely chopped walnuts.

Cream butter; add sugar and cream them together. Add eggs and vanilla. Sift together flour, baking powder, cocoa and salt. Add to mixture alternately with milk. Add rolled cracker crumbs and beat thoroughly. Add cocoanut and nuts. Spread mixture thinly in buttered shallow oblong pan (13 × 9 × 2-inch). Bake in hot oven (375 degrees) for 25 minutes. Cut into squares.
Yield: 3 dozen squares.

MINI CHIP SUGAR COOKIES

¾ cupful granulated sugar . . . ½ cupful light brown sugar, packed . . . ⅓ cupful butter . . . 1 egg . . . 1 teaspoonful vanilla . . . 2 cupfuls flour (all-purpose) . . . 1 teaspoonful baking soda . . . ½ teaspoonful baking powder . . . ½ teaspoonful salt . . . ½ cupful sour milk . . . 2 cupfuls (12-ounce package) Hershey's Mini Chips.

Cream the sugars and the butter until light and fluffy. Add the egg and the vanilla and beat well. Stir together the flour, baking soda, baking powder and salt; add to the creamed mixture alternately with the sour milk. Stir in the Mini Chips. Drop by heaping teaspoonfuls 2 inches apart onto a greased baking sheet. Bake in a moderate oven (350 degrees) 8 to 10 minutes. *Yield: About 2 dozen cookies.*

CHOCOLATE MIDGETS

½ cupful butter . . . ½ cupful (5½-ounce can) Hershey's Chocolate
Flavored Syrup . . . 2 eggs . . . ¾ cupful granulated sugar . . .
¾ cupful flour (all-purpose) . . . ¼ teaspoonful baking powder . . .
1 cupful chopped nutmeats . . . 1 teaspoonful vanilla.

Melt the butter, and mix with the chocolate syrup; set
aside till cool. Beat the eggs without separating; add the
sugar and then beat again. Sprinkle the flour, sifted with
the baking powder, over the nutmeats, and mix all the ingredients together, adding the vanilla. Spread in a greased
and floured shallow pan (9 × 9 × 1¾-inch), and bake
in a moderate oven (350 degrees) about 25 minutes.
Cut into 1-inch squares.
Yield: 3 dozen squares.

COCOA-MOLASSES DROP CAKES

⅓ cupful butter . . . ⅓ cupful granulated sugar . . . ⅓ cupful
molasses . . . 1 egg . . . ⅞ cupful sifted flour (all-purpose)
. . . 1 teaspoonful baking powder . . . 3 tablespoonfuls
Hershey's Cocoa . . . ½ cupful chopped nuts.

Cream butter and sugar; add molasses and the egg.
Sift together flour, baking powder and cocoa; add to the
first mixture. Stir in the nuts, and drop mixture from the
end of a spoon onto greased baking tins (cookie sheets).
Bake in a moderate oven (375 degrees) for 8 to 10 minutes.
Yield: About 2½ dozen cookies.

CHOCOLATE ROBINS

2 squares Hershey's Baking Chocolate . . . ½ cupful butter . . .
3 eggs . . . 1 cupful granulated sugar . . . ¾ cupful flour
(all-purpose) . . . ½ teaspoonful baking powder . . .
½ teaspoonful salt . . . dash cinnamon . . . ¾ cupful chopped
nutmeats . . . ¼ cupful chopped dates or raisins.

Melt baking chocolate and butter in top of double
boiler over simmering water. Beat eggs and sugar, and add
chocolate mixture. Sift flour, baking powder, salt, cinnamon, and add with nuts and dates or raisins. Spread
in a well-greased pan (9 × 9 × 1¾-inch). Bake 25
minutes in moderate oven (350 degrees). Cut into squares.
Yield: 16 robins.

CHOCOLATE SYRUP BROWNIES

1 egg . . . 1 cupful brown sugar, packed . . . ¾ cupful
Hershey's Chocolate Flavored Syrup . . . 1½ cupfuls flour
(all-purpose) . . . ¼ teaspoonful baking soda . . . dash of
salt . . . ½ cupful butter, melted . . . ¾ cupful chopped
pecans or walnuts.

Beat the egg, and add the sugar and chocolate syrup.
Sift the flour, baking soda and salt together, and add to
the sugar mixture. Then fold in the butter and the nutmeats. Spread in a well-greased shallow baking tin (9-inch
square), and bake in a moderate oven (350 degrees) 35
to 40 minutes. Cut while warm into small squares.
Yield: 16 brownies.

CHOCOLATE PINKS
(Small Cupcakes)

3 tablespoonfuls butter . . . ½ cupful granulated sugar . . .
1 egg yolk . . . ½ teaspoonful vanilla . . . ⅔ cupful flour
(all-purpose) . . . ¼ teaspoonful baking soda . . . 3
tablespoonfuls Hershey's Cocoa . . . ½ cupful milk . . . 1
egg white . . . 2 Hershey's Milk Chocolate Bars with Almonds
(1.05 ounces each).

Cream the butter and sugar together; add the egg yolk
and vanilla, and beat well. Sift together flour, baking
soda and cocoa; add with milk to other ingredients. Add
stiffly beaten egg white. Bake in very small buttered tins
(1¾-inch muffin pans) in a moderate oven (350 degrees)
for 15 minutes. Ice with Pink Butter Icing (page 30) and
scatter Hershey's Almond Bars, cut into neat pieces or
grated, over the cakes while icing is still soft.
Yield: About 2 dozen small cupcakes.

Top to bottom:
Chocolate Pinks;
Chocolate Syrup Brownies;
Chocolate Robins

CHOCOLATE DATE AND NUT BARS

2 eggs . . . ½ cupful granulated sugar . . . ½ cupful sifted flour (all-purpose) . . . 1 teaspoonful baking powder . . .
6 tablespoonfuls Hershey's Chocolate Flavored Syrup . . .
1 teaspoonful vanilla . . . ½ cupful walnut nutmeats, chopped . . . ½ cupful dates, chopped.

Beat the eggs thoroughly, and gradually beat in the sugar. Sift the flour and baking powder. Add to the egg and sugar mixture and also add the chocolate syrup and vanilla. Then add the walnut nutmeats and the dates, which have been chopped into small pieces. Beat together and spread in a greased shallow pan (9 × 9 × 1¾-inch). Bake in a moderate oven (350 degrees) 25 minutes. When cool, cut the cake into 1 × 3-inch strips. Sprinkle with 4X sugar (confectioners').
Yield: About 2 dozen bars.

CHOCOLATE ALMOND NUGGETS
(Christmas Cakes)

6 tablespoonfuls butter . . . 1 cupful granulated sugar . . .
1 egg . . . 2 squares Hershey's Baking Chocolate . . .
2 cupfuls sifted flour (all-purpose) . . . 2 teaspoonfuls baking powder . . . dash of salt . . . ½ cupful chopped blanched almonds . . . ¼ cupful milk . . . nutmeats, cherries or raisins.

Cream the butter and sugar, and add the egg, unbeaten, then the baking chocolate, melted over simmering water. Sift the flour, baking powder and salt together. Mix with almonds, blanched and finely chopped. Stir into egg and sugar mixture alternately with the milk. Chill the dough for several hours, then pinch off bits the size of a large marble and press a halved nutmeat or cherry or raisin onto each. Bake in a moderate oven (375 degrees) for 8 to 10 minutes on a greased baking tin (cookie sheet).
Yield: About 4 dozen cookies.

Chocolate Walnut Wheels

CHOCOLATE WALNUT WHEELS

⅓ cupful butter . . . 1 cupful granulated sugar . . . 1 egg . . .
2 squares Hershey's Baking Chocolate, melted . . .
¼ teaspoonful vanilla . . . ⅔ cupful sifted cake flour . . .
¼ teaspoonful salt . . . 1 cupful minced walnuts . . . walnut
halves.

Cream butter, and add sugar gradually. Add egg,
melted baking chocolate and vanilla. Add flour, salt and
nuts, and beat well. Drop from tip of spoon 1 inch apart
onto greased baking sheet. Garnish each with walnut
halves. Bake in moderate oven (350 degrees) 10 minutes.
Yield: 2 dozen wheels.

BLUE RIBBON FRUIT COOKIES

6 tablespoonfuls melted butter . . . ¾ cupful brown sugar, packed . . . 2 eggs . . . 2 squares Hershey's Baking Chocolate, melted . . . 1 cupful flour (all-purpose) . . . 1 teaspoonful baking powder . . . ½ teaspoonful salt . . . ¼ teaspoonful cinnamon . . . ½ cupful seeded raisins . . . ½ cupful candied pineapple, chopped . . . ½ cupful chopped nuts.

Cream butter and sugar; add eggs. Add melted baking chocolate, and beat thoroughly. Combine the flour, baking powder, salt and cinnamon. Add to the mixture, and beat well. Add the raisins, pineapple and nuts. Drop (the size of a silver dollar) from teaspoon onto a greased baking sheet. Bake in a moderate oven (350 degrees) for 10 minutes.

Yield: 2 dozen large cookies.

CHOCOLATE COCOANUT MACAROONS

1 square Hershey's Baking Chocolate . . . ⅔ cupful sweetened condensed milk . . . 1½ cupfuls shredded cocoanut . . . ½ teaspoonful vanilla.

Melt the baking chocolate in a double boiler over simmering water. Add the condensed milk and blend. Add the cocoanut and vanilla. Drop (size of half dollar) onto buttered baking sheet. Bake in a moderate oven (350 degrees) 15 minutes. Watch cookies carefully for overbaking. Remove immediately from baking sheet.

Yield: 2 dozen macaroons.

COCOA BREAD CRUMB COOKIES

¼ cupful butter . . . ½ cupful granulated sugar . . . ¼ cupful Hershey's Cocoa . . . 2 eggs . . . 1 teaspoonful vanilla . . . 1 cupful fine bread crumbs.

Cream the butter, sugar and cocoa together thoroughly. Add the eggs and vanilla, then the crumbs. (The mixture should be as thick as cake batter.) Spread thin in a well-greased cake pan (8 × 8 × 2-inch), and bake in a slow oven (300 degrees) for 20 minutes. Cut into squares or rounds, and put together sandwich fashion with favorite jelly or jam. Ice lightly with any plain or chocolate icing.

Yield: 2 dozen squares.

CHOCOLATE FRUIT COOKIES

1 cupful shortening . . . 2 cupfuls brown sugar, packed . . .
2 eggs . . . 1 cupful milk . . . 2 teaspoonfuls baking soda
. . . 3 cupfuls flour (all-purpose) . . . ½ cupful Hershey's
Cocoa . . . 1 cupful raisins . . . 1 cupful walnut nutmeats.

Cream the shortening with the sugar. Add the eggs
and the milk, in which the baking soda has been dissolved.
Then add the flour and cocoa, and blend well. Add the
raisins and walnut nutmeats. Drop mixture from the end
of a spoon onto well-greased cookie sheets. Bake in a
moderate oven (375 degrees) for 8 to 10 minutes. Ice
with double recipe of Vanilla Butter Icing (page 30).
Yield: 9 dozen cookies.

CHOCOLATETOWN CHIP COOKIES

¾ cupful butter . . . ½ cupful granulated sugar . . . 1 cupful
brown sugar, packed . . . 1 teaspoonful vanilla . . . 2
eggs . . . 2 cupfuls flour (all-purpose) . . . 1 teaspoonful
baking soda . . . 1 teaspoonful salt . . . 2 cupfuls (12-ounce
package) Hershey's Baking Chips.

Cream the butter, sugars and vanilla until light and
fluffy. Add the eggs and beat well. Sift together the flour,
baking soda and salt; add to the creamed mixture. Add
the baking pieces and blend well. Drop by teaspoonfuls
onto lightly greased baking sheet. Bake in a moderate
oven (375 degrees) 8 to 10 minutes.
Yield: About 8 dozen cookies.

COCOA CANDY CAKES

⅓ cupful butter . . . 3 tablespoonfuls Hershey's Cocoa . . .
1 cupful granulated sugar . . . 1 egg . . . ½ teaspoonful
vanilla . . . ½ cupful flour (all-purpose) . . . dash of salt . . .
½ cupful chopped walnuts or other nutmeats.

Melt butter and add cocoa. Gradually add sugar, then
the egg, slightly beaten, the vanilla, then the flour and
salt mixed together and the nutmeats. Spread mixture in
a well-greased pan (8 × 8 × 2-inch), and bake in a
moderate oven (350 degrees) for 25 minutes. Frost with
Chocolate Butter Icing (page 34) while still warm. Cut
into squares while still warm, but cool in pan.
Yield: 16 candy cakes.

Candies

COUNTRY CLUB TWO-STORY FUDGE

First Story:

2¼ cupfuls granulated sugar . . . 1 cupful milk . . . 3 squares Hershey's Baking Chocolate . . . 1 tablespoonful light corn syrup . . . 2 tablespoonfuls butter . . . 1 teaspoonful vanilla . . . ½ cupful chopped nutmeats.

Combine sugar, milk, the baking chocolate, broken into small pieces, and the corn syrup in a heavy saucepan (3-quart). Place over medium heat and stir gently till baking chocolate is melted, then cook with very little stirring to soft-ball stage (234° F.). Remove from the fire; add butter and vanilla. Cool, undisturbed, to lukewarm (110° F.). Beat vigorously until fudge thickens and starts to lose its gloss; add nuts and quickly pour into a buttered 9 × 9 × 1¾-inch pan. Set aside to cool.

Second Story:

2½ cupfuls granulated sugar . . . ½ cupful light cream . . . ½ cupful milk . . . ¼ teaspoonful salt . . . 1 tablespoonful light corn syrup . . . 2 tablespoonfuls butter . . . 1 teaspoonful vanilla . . . ⅓ cupful chopped glace cherries.

Butter sides of a heavy saucepan (2-quart). In it combine sugar, cream, milk, salt and corn syrup. Place over medium heat, and stir until sugar is dissolved, then cook to soft-ball stage (236° F.). Remove from fire; add butter and vanilla. Cool, undisturbed, to lukewarm (110° F.). Beat vigorously until mixture becomes very thick and starts to lose its gloss. Quickly stir in glace cherries, and pour over the dark fudge, smoothing the surface with a knife. Cut into squares while still warm.

Yield: 4 dozen pieces.

CHOCOLATE LOG CABIN ROLLS

1 cupful light brown sugar, packed . . . ¾ cupful granulated
sugar . . . ½ cupful maple syrup . . . 1 cupful light cream . . .
2 tablespoonfuls butter . . . few grains salt . . . 1½ squares
Hershey's Baking Chocolate . . . 1 egg white . . . 1 cupful
broken pecans.

Combine sugars, maple syrup, cream, butter, salt and
the baking chocolate, broken into small pieces, in a heavy
saucepan (3-quart). Bring gently to boiling point, stirring
constantly. Cover and cook 5 minutes. Remove cover
and cook, stirring occasionally, until mixture forms soft
ball in cold water (236° F.). Cool until bottom of pan
feels lukewarm (110° F.). Beat vigorously until fudge
begins to lose its gloss and holds its shape. Turn out onto
a buttered surface. Knead fudge till it can be shaped,
keeping hands well-buttered. Shape into two 9-inch rolls;
brush with slightly beaten egg white. Roll immediately
in broken pecans, pressing nuts into roll to coat. Wrap
and chill until ready to slice.
Yield: About 36 slices.

CHOCOLATE PECAN PRALINES

1 cupful granulated sugar . . . 1 cupful light brown sugar or
maple sugar, packed . . . ½ cupful light cream . . .
¼ teaspoonful salt . . . 2 squares Hershey's Baking Chocolate
. . . 1 tablespoonful butter . . . 1 cupful coarsely chopped
pecans . . . 1 teaspoonful vanilla.

Combine sugars, cream and salt in a large saucepan.
Cook over medium heat, stirring constantly, to 228° F. on
candy thermometer. Remove from heat, and add the
baking chocolate, broken into small pieces, the butter
and pecans. Return to heat; stirring constantly, cook to
soft-ball stage (234° F.). Remove from heat; flavor with
vanilla, and cool 5 minutes. Beat 10 to 15 seconds or until
slightly thickened. Quickly drop candy by large spoonfuls
onto greased plates (or waxed paper). If mixture becomes
too thick to drop, stir in a tablespoonful of hot water.
Yield: About 2 dozen pieces.

CHOCOLATE COCOANUT SQUARES

⅓ cupful light corn syrup . . . 2 tablespoonfuls water . . .
2 tablespoonfuls granulated sugar . . . 2¼ cupfuls (7-ounce
can) flaked cocoanut . . . 1 teaspoonful vanilla . . . ¾ cupful
Hershey's Baking Chips . . . ⅓ cupful toasted slivered
almonds or chopped pecans.

Cook the corn syrup, water and sugar together in a
small saucepan over medium heat to the soft-ball stage
(234° F.). Remove from heat; add cocoanut and vanilla,
stirring to blend well. Put into an 8-inch square pan.
Melt baking pieces in top of double boiler over hot,
not boiling, water. Pour over cocoanut; spread with
spatula and sprinkle with nuts. Cool. Cut into squares.
Yield: 3 dozen squares.

CHOCOLATE NUT CLUSTERS

1 cupful (5¾-ounce package) Hershey's Milk Chocolate Chips
. . . 1 teaspoonful shortening . . . cashews, peanuts, pecan
halves, English walnut halves or miniature marshmallows.

Pick over the nutmeats. Melt the chocolate pieces with
shortening in top of double boiler over hot, not boiling,
water. Throw in half a cupful of nuts (one kind at a
time), and stir around in the melted chocolate. Take out
nuts with a fork, and place in little piles on waxed paper-
covered cookie sheet. Refrigerate until set.

FUDGE CARAMELS

⅔ cupful Hershey's Cocoa . . . 2 cupfuls granulated sugar
. . . 1 cupful light corn syrup . . . ⅛ teaspoonful salt . . .
1 cupful evaporated milk . . . ½ cupful water . . . ¼ cupful
butter . . . 1 teaspoonful vanilla.

Combine cocoa, sugar, corn syrup and salt in a heavy
saucepan (3-quart). Add evaporated milk and water.
Bring to a boil over medium heat, stirring constantly.
Cook, stirring frequently, until mixture forms a firm ball
in cold water (245° F.). Remove from fire; drop in butter
and vanilla, stirring to completely blend in butter. Pour
into buttered 9-inch square pan. Cool. Cut into squares
(scissors are helpful), and wrap in waxed paper.
Yield: About 6 dozen caramels.

Chocolate Cocoanut Squares

ANGEL FUDGE

2 cupfuls granulated sugar . . . 1 cupful Hershey's Chocolate Flavored Syrup . . . 1 cupful milk . . . 1 tablespoonful butter . . . 1 teaspoonful vanilla . . . ¾ cupful marshmallow whip.

Place the sugar, chocolate syrup and milk in a deep kettle (3-quart saucepan), and stir over medium heat until the ingredients are well blended. Boil, without stirring, until the mixture forms a soft ball (234° F.) when dropped into cold water. Remove from fire, and add the butter, vanilla and marshmallow whip. Do not stir. Cool undisturbed until the mixture has cooled to lukewarm (110° F.). Then beat vigorously until fudge loses gloss (fudge will hold shape). Pour into buttered 8-inch square pan. Cut into squares while warm.
Yield: 3 dozen pieces.

CHOCOLATE SEAFOAM

2 cupfuls light brown sugar, packed . . . ¾ cupful cold water
. . . ½ cupful (5½-ounce can) Hershey's Chocolate Flavored
Syrup . . . 2 egg whites . . . 1 teaspoonful vanilla . . .
1 square Hershey's Baking Chocolate, melted . . . ½ cupful
nutmeats.

Mix together sugar, water and chocolate syrup in a
heavy saucepan (3-quart). Cook over medium heat,
stirring constantly, till sugar dissolves and mixture boils.
Then cook to hard-ball stage (250° F.) without stirring.
Remove pan from heat.

Immediately beat egg whites till stiff. Pour hot syrup
in a thin stream over beaten egg whites, beating constantly at high speed on mixer. Continue beating till
mixture forms peaks when dropped from spoon, about
10 minutes. Quickly stir in vanilla and melted baking
chocolate by hand. Blend in nutmeats. Drop by teaspoonfuls onto waxed paper. Cool.

Yield: 3 to 4 dozen pieces.

CHOCOLATE CHIP-PEANUT BUTTER FUDGE

2 cupfuls granulated sugar . . . ⅔ cupful milk . . .
2 tablespoonfuls light corn syrup . . . 1 tablespoonful butter
. . . 1 teaspoonful vanilla . . . ½ cupful peanut butter . . .
1 cupful (5¾-ounce package) Hershey's Milk Chocolate Chips.

Combine sugar, milk and corn syrup in a heavy saucepan (3-quart); bring to a boil, stirring constantly, until
mixture boils. Continue boiling without stirring to the
soft-ball stage (234° F.). Remove from heat. Add butter
without stirring, and cool to lukewarm (110° F.).

Add vanilla and peanut butter; beat until mixture begins to thicken and lose its gloss. (Watch carefully, this
fudge has a short beating time.) *Quickly* add chocolate
pieces, and turn into buttered 8 × 8 × 2-inch pan.
While warm, mark into squares. Cool until firm, then
cut as marked.

Yield: About 3 dozen squares.

Left to right:
Angel Fudge;
Chocolate Seafoam;
Chocolate Chip-Peanut Butter Fudge

CHOCOLATE POPCORN BALLS

1¼ cupfuls granulated sugar . . . ½ cupful Hershey's Cocoa
. . . ¾ cupful light corn syrup . . . 2 teaspoonfuls cider vinegar
. . . ⅛ teaspoonful salt . . . 2 tablespoonfuls butter . . .
¼ cupful evaporated milk . . . 2 quarts popped corn.

Mix together the sugar, cocoa, corn syrup, vinegar and salt thoroughly in a heavy saucepan. Add butter; cook slowly, stirring constantly, until the sugar dissolves. Bring the mixture to a boil; add evaporated milk slowly so boiling does not stop. Cook mixture over low fire, stirring occasionally, until it reaches 265° F. Mix into 2 quarts freshly popped corn. Dip out large spoonfuls and make into balls, first wetting the hands in cold water or rubbing them lightly with butter. One must work quickly.
Yield: Twenty 4-inch balls.
Variation: Add ¼ cupful chopped nutmeats to chocolate mixture before mixing into popped corn.

CHOCOLATE TURKISH PASTE
(Gumdrop-like Confection)

3 tablespoonfuls granulated gelatin (unflavored) . . . ½ cupful
cold water . . . 2 cupfuls granulated sugar . . . ⅓ cupful
Hershey's Cocoa . . . ⅔ cupful water . . . 1 teaspoonful vanilla.

Soak the gelatin in ½ cupful cold water 10 minutes. Combine sugar, cocoa and ⅔ cupful water in a heavy saucepan; cook, stirring constantly, until the sugar is well dissolved. Blend in the gelatin and bring to a boil; cook slowly over a low fire about 15 minutes (220° F.) without stirring. Remove from fire; stir in the vanilla, and cool undisturbed for about 30 minutes. Line the bottom of a shallow pan (8-inch square) with waxed paper. Pour in cooled mixture. Let stand 24 hours, then invert onto a well-sugared surface. Carefully peel off paper; cut into squares and roll in granulated sugar.
Yield: About 4 dozen squares.

CHOCOLATE CHERRY CORDIALS

Centers:

¼ cupful butter . . . 2 to 2 ¼ cupfuls 4X sugar (confectioners')
. . . 1 tablespoonful milk . . . ½ teaspoonful vanilla . . .
⅛ teaspoonful almond extract . . . about 3 dozen
maraschino cherries, drained.

Thoroughly cream butter with sugar and milk. Blend in vanilla and almond extract. (If mixture is too sticky, additional sugar may be added.) Mold a small amount around a cherry, being careful to completely cover each cherry. Place on waxed paper-covered tray, set aside.

Coating:

2 cupfuls (12-ounce package) Hershey's Mini Chips or Baking Chips . . . 2 tablespoonfuls shortening (not butter or margarine).

Completely melt chips and shortening in top of double boiler over hot, not boiling water. Cool, stirring occasionally, until coating is lukewarm and slightly thickened (98° F); maintain temperature while dipping.

Dipping:

Drop centers into coating mixture; roll to coat completely and remove with fork. Draw fork across rim of pan to remove excess coating. Drop from fork upside down onto waxed paper, swirling "thread" of coating from fork across top for a decorative touch. Allow coating to become firm at room temperature; check bottoms and reseal with additional melted coating if necessary. Store in a cool place (do not refrigerate) at least two days to form cordial.

Yield: About 3 dozen candies.

CHOCOLATE PEANUT BUTTER FUDGE

2 cupfuls granulated sugar . . . ⅔ cupful milk . . . 3 squares Hershey's Baking Chocolate . . . 1 cupful marshmallow whip . . . ¾ cupful peanut butter . . . 1 teaspoonful vanilla.

Combine sugar, milk and the baking chocolate, broken into small pieces, in a heavy saucepan. Cook over medium heat, stirring constantly, until mixture boils. Cook to the soft-ball stage (234° F.) without stirring. Remove from heat, and add marshmallow whip, peanut butter and vanilla. Stir just until blended. Pour into buttered 9 × 9 × 1¾-inch pan. Cool and cut into squares.

Yield: About 3 dozen squares.

CHOCOLATE COCOANUT BALLS

3 squares Hershey's Baking Chocolate . . . ¼ cupful butter . . . ½ cupful sweetened condensed milk . . . ¾ cupful granulated sugar . . . ¼ cupful water . . . 1 tablespoonful corn syrup . . . 1 teaspoonful vanilla . . . 2 cupfuls (7-ounce can) shredded cocoanut . . . 1 cupful chopped nuts . . . 4X sugar (confectioners').

Melt baking chocolate with butter in top of double boiler over simmering water. Add condensed milk and blend well. In saucepan cook granulated sugar, water and corn syrup, stirring until sugar is dissolved. Boil to firm-ball stage (250° F.). Remove from heat and stir into chocolate mixture. Blend in vanilla, cocoanut and chopped nuts. Chill until firm enough to handle. Form mixture into 1-inch balls and roll in 4X sugar.

Yield: About 4 dozen candies.

CREAMY COCOA TAFFY

1¼ cupfuls granulated sugar . . . ⅓ cupful Hershey's Cocoa
. . . ¾ cupful light corn syrup . . . 2 teaspoonfuls cider
vinegar . . . ⅛ teaspoonful salt . . . 1 tablespoonful butter . . .
¼ cupful evaporated milk.

Combine the sugar and cocoa thoroughly in a heavy
saucepan. Add the corn syrup, vinegar and salt; blend
well. Bring the mixture to a boil over medium heat,
stirring constantly, then add the butter and stir in the
evaporated milk slowly so the boiling does not stop.
Cook mixture over medium heat, stirring occasionally,
until the temperature reaches 248° F. Immediately pour
into a buttered pan. Cool until it can be handled and
pull, a portion at a time, until candy is lighter in color.
Cut with scissors into 1-inch pieces. Wrap in waxed paper.
Yield: 6 dozen pieces.

CHOCOLATE POTATO CANDY

1 medium baked potato, mashed (¾ cupful) . . . ½ teaspoonful
salt . . . 1 teaspoonful vanilla . . . ⅓ cupful Hershey's Cocoa
. . . about 4½ cupfuls 4X sugar (confectioners') . . . Chocolate
Glaze (page 37).

Combine the mashed potato, salt and vanilla. Gradually
beat in the cocoa and sugar until the mixture is stiff
enough to be rolled into balls. Chill the balls then coat
with the chocolate given in the Chocolate Cherry Cordials
recipe (page 85).
Yield: 4 dozen candies.

Beverages

Left to right:
Orange Chocolate Float (page 90);
Frosted Chocolate Shake (page 90)

FROSTED CHOCOLATE SHAKE

2 to 3 tablespoonfuls Hershey's Chocolate Flavored Syrup . . .
¾ cupful chilled milk . . . 1 teaspoonful granulated sugar . . .
½ teaspoonful vanilla . . . ½ cupful vanilla ice cream.

Combine chocolate syrup, milk, sugar and vanilla in shaker or glass jar; shake vigorously. Add ice cream and shake again. Serve immediately, pouring into tall glass. Garnish with maraschino cherry or spray of mint.
Yield: One 10-ounce serving.

ORANGE CHOCOLATE FLOAT

½ glass (½ cupful) orange juice . . . 1 tablespoonful granulated sugar . . . 2 tablespoonfuls Hershey's Chocolate Flavored Syrup . . . 1 egg white, beaten stiff (optional) . . . whipped cream.

Combine orange juice, sugar and chocolate syrup; shake vigorously. Add beaten egg white, if desired, and shake again. Pour over crushed ice in glass and top with whipped cream. Garnish with an orange slice.
Yield: One 8-ounce serving.

COCOMOKO FLOAT

¼ cupful clear black coffee . . . 3 tablespoonfuls Hershey's Chocolate Flavored Syrup . . . 2 teaspoonfuls granulated sugar or more, as desired . . . ½ teaspoonful vanilla . . . ½ cupful milk . . . whipped cream.

Mix all ingredients together except whipped cream, and shake vigorously. Pour into a tall glass one-fourth filled with crushed ice. Beat well and top with a spoonful of whipped cream.
Yield: One 8-ounce serving.

CHOCOLATE PINEAPPLE FREEZE

¼ cupful water . . . 3 tablespoonfuls Hershey's Chocolate Flavored Syrup . . . ¾ cupful juice from canned pineapple.

Mix all the ingredients together, and beat or shake to a foam. Serve in a tall ice-filled glass with a straw.
Yield: 1 tall glass.

Left to right:
Cocomoko Float;
Chocolate Pineapple Freeze;
Rich Iced Chocolate

RICH ICED CHOCOLATE

4 squares Hershey's Baking Chocolate . . . 1 quart hot water
. . . dash of salt . . . 1 cupful granulated sugar . . .
1 teaspoonful vanilla . . . pint of heavy cream.

Break the baking chocolate into small pieces; add to
the hot water with the salt and sugar. Boil all together
5 minutes, then cool and add vanilla. Whip the cream
partially; pour the chocolate over it and beat with a
rotary beater to a light froth. Pour into glasses half filled
with crushed ice. If desired, top with whipped cream.
Yield: Six 8-ounce servings.

CHOCOLATE SYRUP ICED CHOCOLATE

1½ cupfuls (1-pound can) Hershey's Chocolate Flavored
Syrup . . . 1 quart cold milk . . . 1 teaspoonful vanilla . . .
1 pint heavy cream.

Blend together chocolate syrup, cold milk and vanilla.
Whip the cream partially; pour the chocolate over it and
beat to a light froth. Pour into glasses half filled with
crushed ice. If desired, top each glass with whipped cream.
Yield: Three 8-ounce servings.

HOT COCOA

2 tablespoonfuls Hershey's Cocoa . . . 3 tablespoonfuls
granulated sugar . . . dash of salt . . . ¼ cupful hot water . . .
1½ cupfuls milk . . . marshmallows or marshmallow whip.

Blend the cocoa, sugar and salt in a 1½-quart saucepan,
and gradually add the hot water. Boil over medium heat
for 2 minutes, stirring constantly. Add the milk and heat
thoroughly, stirring occasionally. *Do not boil.* Remove from
heat and beat with a rotary beater until foamy. Serve
hot. Top with marshmallows or marshmallow whip.
Yield: About three 6-ounce servings.

HOT COCOA FOR A CROWD

1¼ cupfuls Hershey's Cocoa . . . 1½ cupfuls granulated
sugar . . . ¾ teaspoonful salt . . . 1¾ cupfuls hot water . . .
4 quarts milk . . . 1 tablespoonful vanilla.

Blend the cocoa, sugar and salt in a 6-quart saucepan,
and gradually add the hot water. Boil over medium heat
for 2 minutes, stirring constantly. Add the milk and
heat thoroughly, stirring occasionally. *Do not boil.* Remove
from heat and add vanilla. Beat with a rotary beater until
foamy. Serve hot and garnish with whipped cream,
marshmallows, marshmallow whip, dash of cinnamon or
cinnamon sticks.
Yield: 4½ quarts or twenty four 6-ounce servings.

MULLED COCOA CUP

2 quarts milk . . . 1 teaspoonful cinnamon . . . ½ teaspoonful
nutmeg . . . ¼ teaspoonful cloves . . . ½ cupful Hershey's
Cocoa . . . 1 cupful granulated sugar . . . ½ teaspoonful salt
. . . 4 cupfuls boiling water . . . 2 teaspoonfuls vanilla or
1 teaspoonful almond extract . . . shredded almonds.

Scald milk with cinnamon, nutmeg and cloves. Mix
cocoa, sugar and salt; add to boiling water. Boil 5 minutes. Combine mixtures; add vanilla or almond extract,
and beat 2 minutes until frothy. Pour into mugs, sprinkle
with nuts and serve instantly.
Yield: Sixteen 6-ounce servings.

FIVE O'CLOCK WHIPPED CHOCOLATE

2 tablespoonfuls Hershey's Cocoa . . . 3 tablespoonfuls granulated sugar . . . dash of salt . . . ¼ cupful hot water . . . 1½ cupfuls milk . . . 2 tablespoonfuls marshmallow whip . . . few drops of vanilla.

Prepare the chocolate in the usual way. (Blend the cocoa, sugar and salt in a 1½-quart saucepan, and gradually add the hot water. Boil over medium heat for 2 minutes, stirring constantly. Add the milk and heat thoroughly, stirring occasionally. *Do not boil.* Remove from heat and beat with a rotary beater until foamy*.) Then the marshmallow whip may be beaten into it. Flavor with a few drops of vanilla.

Yield: Two 8-ounce servings.

*Beating the chocolate prevents the formation of a skin over the surface, caused by the coagulation of particles of albumen during the scalding process. Beating also adds greatly to the smoothness of the drink.

ROYAL HOT CHOCOLATE

2 squares Hershey's Baking Chocolate . . . 1¼ cupfuls (14-ounce can) sweetened condensed milk . . . 4 cupfuls boiling water . . . few grains salt . . . 1 teaspoonful vanilla . . . whipped cream . . . cinnamon.

Melt baking chocolate in top of double boiler over simmering water. Add condensed milk, and add boiling water gradually while stirring constantly. Add salt and vanilla. Serve in cups with spoonful of whipped cream dusted with cinnamon.

Yield: Seven 6-ounce servings.

CHOCOLATE MALTED MILK

3 tablespoonfuls Hershey's Chocolate Flavored Syrup . . . 2 to 3 teaspoonfuls malted milk powder . . . 1 cupful chilled milk.

Mix chocolate syrup, malted milk powder and milk. Shake vigorously or beat until frothy. Serve cold.

Yield: One 8-ounce serving.

SPANISH CHOCOLATE

4 Hershey's Milk Chocolate Bars (1.05 ounces each) . . .
2 cupfuls light cream . . . ¼ cupful clear black coffee . . .
whipped cream.

Melt the milk chocolate bars in the cream over low
heat, stirring constantly. Stir in the coffee, and beat with
a rotary beater to a heavy froth. Serve hot with a dab of
whipped cream or pour over crushed ice and top with
whipped cream.
Yield: Four 5-ounce servings.

CHOCOLATE EGG NOG

½ square Hershey's Baking Chocolate . . . 2 tablespoonfuls
granulated sugar . . . 2 tablespoonfuls water . . .
1 tablespoonful malted milk powder . . . 1 egg . . . milk.

Mix the baking chocolate, broken into small pieces,
sugar and water together, and cook in top of double
boiler over simmering water till baking chocolate is melted.
Add the malted milk powder and the egg, and beat till
light and frothy. Pour over crushed ice in a glass and fill
with milk. Beat a moment before serving. This is a very
nutritious drink.
Yield: One 8-ounce serving.

MINT COCOA CUP

1 quart milk . . . ¾ cupful granulated sugar . . .
6 tablespoonfuls Hershey's Cocoa . . . 1 cupful boiling water
. . . ⅛ teaspoonful mint extract or 3 sprays fresh mint*
. . . whipped cream.

Scald milk with sugar and cocoa. Add boiling water
and beat with a rotary beater. Cool. Add mint extract*.
Pour over crushed ice; top with a spoonful of whipped
cream and garnish with a spray of mint.
Yield: Five 8-ounce servings.
*When using fresh mint, crush the mint, steep 10 minutes in
the 1 cupful boiling water and remove mint. Add to scalded
milk in place of boiling water.*